WORLD LEADERS I HAVE KNOWN

Jerome Davis

WORLD

LEADERS

I HAVE

KNOWN

New York: THE CITADEL PRESS

49206

DEDICATED *to all those who forget themselves and the self-center and devote their lives to the welfare of humanity. Let us try to understand people who are different from ourselves, and help them—not try to exterminate them.*

Let us, here and now, respond to the challenge of the lives of the leaders we meet here. Let us, too, devote our lives not to material possessions but to the service of every race and people, recognizing that we are all brothers in one small world.

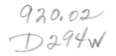

FOREWORD

My acquaintance with Jerome Davis began in our student days at Union Theological Seminary. His crusading passion was evident even then. He was reared in a family filled with missionary spirit. He is still aglow with zeal for a better world.

Few men of my acquaintance have managed to be in so many of the world's hot spots. To have been present in Russia when Lenin was rising to power, and to have had personal contact with him—from such a launching pad Jerome Davis has orbited the globe, not a hundred miles above the earth like an astronaut, but close in amidst its tensions.

Dr. Davis views intently, feels intensely, and writes interestingly. I have not had occasion to corroborate his facts and I assume no responsibility for endorsing all his conclusions. Some of the world leaders he describes have also been known to me. I share his high estimate of such men as Harry Emerson Fosdick and Stephen Wise, whom I too have counted as friends. His treatment of the known inclines me to have confidence in his appraisal of those unknown to me.

One appreciates the author's attempted fairness of judgment in paragraphs like this: "While I differed with Lenin in his faith in the materialistic philosophy of Karl Marx and in the dictatorship of the Communist party, I agreed with Abramovitch, the famous Menshevist leader who, although in opposition to Lenin, wrote, 'It would be mistaken to imagine Lenin as a demoniacal being. On the contrary, his home life and personal relations would merit the enthusiasm of any Baptist minister. It is difficult to conceive a simpler, kinder, and more unpretentious person than Lenin at home.' "

The list of personalities portrayed reveals that Davis is a liberal. He has been attracted to leaders whom he thought to be fighting for the "underdog." If it be said that he is too generous in his judging the motives of the "leftists," it should be remembered how many agitators are making money catering to the fears and suspicions of the "rightists."

And one who calls himself a Christian can hardly quarrel with the criteria which Dr. Davis declares as his basis for judging the persons he portrays: "In our appraisal of anyone, anywhere, our first question should be: What were the factors and characteristics of his background, social and personal? What conditioned his development? As far as one can determine, what are his objectives; is he sincere and honest? And to puncture our own self-righteousness, in judging other human beings: 'What would I have been like, what would I have accomplished, had I been born in his place and with his handicaps?' "

The reader should remember that the pictures of the world leaders in this book are portraits rather than photographs. Others may paint them quite differently. Only the Creator can give the final awards for correctness.

Personally I am glad to have viewed Jerome Davis' gallery of portraits.

RALPH W. SOCKMAN

CONTENTS

WORLD LEADERS I HAVE KNOWN

I

INSPIRATION AND DEDICATION

I WAS BORN in Japan and received my first inspiration from both my father and my mother. I don't think I have ever met anyone who was more dedicated than my mother. She was always giving her time, her energy, and her life for others. I never can remember my mother being angry with anyone. She was always trying to help them. Her spirit was etched into my life, and no mother could have done more to help her son than she did.

My father, too, was a devoted and sincere follower of Christ, but he was much more apt to get angry and cross under the strain of long years of service in Japan. Nevertheless, his life made a deep impression upon me.

My father decided early to give his life in service for others. He was born on a farm but managed to work his way through Beloit College. When the Civil War broke out, he felt he should volunteer to help free the slaves. He went in as a private in the 52nd Volunteer Illinois Infantry. He was soon promoted to Color Bearer. My father was strongly opposed to liquor drinking, and when he found the soldiers were indulging and even getting drunk, he put up a big sign in the camp on one of the trees: *Death to the Bottle.* All that happened as a result of this sign was that the soldiers tore it down and were angry at him for putting it up. My father realized that he must use other tactics which would be more effective. He organized a prayer circle, and this began to have some influence on the regiment.

In the Battle of Shiloh the bullets were flying thick and fast, and since Father was carrying the American flag, many were directed at him. My father got behind a tree where he could poke the flag out, and all was well until other soldiers began lining up behind him. My father soon realized that since the flag was drawing bullets, sooner or later some of the men behind him would be shot. He felt it would be wrong to jeopardize their lives. He stepped out from behind the tree, and within one minute was shot. In the hospital, the surgeon wanted to amputate his leg, but my father refused to allow it. The result was that he saved his leg. My father became so popular with his men that when the colonel of the regiment was killed, he was elected lieutenant colonel.

When the war was over, my father completed his theological training. He then went to the Home Mission Board and asked to be sent to the most difficult and needy spot in all America. The Board asked him how much salary he wanted, and he replied, "This is not important for me." "All right," they said, "why don't you go to Cheyenne, Wyoming? There are no churches, but, instead, rows of gambling dens and houses of prostitution."

My father accepted the challenge and went to Wyoming. He helped to build the Congregational church with his own hands. He then helped to build the first sewer in town. Later the governor of the state appointed him superintendent of schools without salary. When there were three churches in Cheyenne, my father decided it was time to go to a more difficult field, so he applied for missionary service. He was sent to Japan and arrived in 1872 when it meant death to be a Christian. There were billboards all over the country stating that anyone who became a Christian would be executed. My father had to hold his prayer meetings with the Japanese late at night, with watchers on the street to let them know if the police were coming. His first convert died in prison, and another was arrested; a letter was delivered to my father saying he would be murdered if he tried to start a Christian school.

Today our Christian practice has deteriorated so far that we will not even permit a United States citizen to go to Red China, but in those days we were more tolerant. My father stayed on in Japan and helped to start Doshisha University in Kyoto, which now has over twenty thousand students.

We think of ourselves as civilized, but are we? Three-fourths of the human race are hungry, diseased and ignorant, and we spend over six million dollars an hour in the United States for armaments. We claim we are not like the savages who murdered each other but we do not hesitate to prepare weapons of destruction that would annihilate the human race. The leaders described in this book have all taken action against the evils of society as they saw them.

It is my belief that we all gain inspiration from the lives of sincere and dedicated individuals. It is for this reason that the achievements of great men should remind us that we can make our lives socially significant. Even when we disagree with the actions of a leader, we should ask ourselves if we would have done better had we been born in his place and brought up in the conditions he experienced. Rather than try to kill people who are different from ourselves, we should try to understand them.

When we think of great leaders like Albert Schweitzer,

our hearts and minds are fired with enthusiasm to go and do likewise in our own feeble way. We begin to realize that we can't have genuine love in our hearts unless and until we put it into practice. When Schweitzer first started for Africa over a half century ago, he was asked this question, "Why would a man with so much to give to the world go and bury himself among a handful of African natives?" Today the whole world knows the answer. He has been serving humanity and lighting a flaming torch of unselfish service for others to follow.

As James Russell Lowell once said, "Not failure but low aim is crime." True leadership is a shining example for us all to follow. We do not have to make the whole world go right, only to do our best to help others and build a world of love and goodwill. In other words, we will never build a world of peace if we sit with folded hands. We must do what many of the leaders in this book have done: work with all our strength, with all our hearts, and with all our minds to promote justice, freedom and love throughout the world.

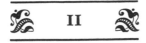

II

TOYOHIKO KAGAWA

JAPAN WAS a military fortress with an Emperor who was a supreme dictator and supposed to be a god. Prostitution was everywhere and the wealthy aristocrats had many concubines. How do you change such a society? Here is the story of a good friend of mine, the child of a concubine who gives the answer in the story of his life.

Kagawa has always been an inspiration to countless people. Since I was born in Japan I was especially interested in his life and work. Here was the son of a wealthy samurai and his geisha concubine. His father died when he was four years old and his mother two months later. He was sent to live with the legal wife of his father who had no children. He did well in his studies and when he moved to Tokushima to live with his brother, who was sixteen years older, he was one of a hundred and fifty who passed the examinations for the Middle School out of three hundred who had tried.

Fortunately for him he started taking English lessons from an American missionary every Tuesday evening. This was to improve his pronunciation since the teachers of English in the school he attended were Japanese. His older brother permitted him to take this extra work but warned him, "Don't start believing in their religion. It's a bad religion." After taking these lessons for some time, Dr. Myers who was a missionary in Tokushima invited

Kagawa to come to his home and read any of the books in his library. Here he read Kant's *Critique of Pure Reason,* Darwin's *Origin of Species* and books about Schopenhauer, Hegel and Tolstoy.

When he was fifteen years of age, his older brother died. He had been dissipating and living an extravagant, wild life beyond his means. Kagawa was then taken into the home of his uncle, a very wealthy man who was president of both a railway and a steamship company.

By this time Toyohiko Kagawa had been influenced somewhat by the American missionaries. Early in the morning he might meditate at the altar of Buddha, but at other times he would repeat verses from the New Testament that Dr. Myers had taught him. After he was in bed at night he would sometimes say this prayer, "Oh God, make me like Christ. Amen."

The Russian Tolstoy also influenced Kagawa. He was impressed by the fact that Tolstoy gave up his wealth and lived a life of poverty and also that he was opposed to the use of force and violence.

When Japan declared war on Russia, military drills were introduced into the Middle School where Kagawa was studying in spite of the fact that the students were too young to go to war. The students were all given guns and had to practice drills.

Kagawa remembered the Bible verse "Love your enemies and pray for those who persecute you." Suddenly Kagawa threw away his gun. The angry teacher commanded, "Pick up your gun." But Kagawa remained motionless.

"Why do you refuse to obey?" the teacher shouted.

Calmly Kawaga replied, "Because I think Japan is making a mistake in going to war."

The teacher became very angry and began beating Kagawa over the head. He fell to the ground with his nose bleeding. Kawaga's action antagonized some of his schoolmates, but he was permitted to continue his classes and in March 1905 he was graduated while the war was still raging.

After graduation his wealthy uncle called him into his room to find out what he planned to do next. Kagawa replied that he intended to become a Christian minister. This was too much for his uncle who became enraged and ordered him to leave the house forever. Kagawa departed carrying his few possessions with him.

Dr. Myers, the American missionary, helped him, and he went on to Meji Seminary in Tokyo. Here many of the students were amazed to find he was opposed to the Japanese war against Russia. Once late at night he was summoned to go to the playground. There some seniors demanded to know if it were true that he was opposed to the war against Russia. Kagawa reiterated his stand. Immediately the students struck him. Kagawa did not retaliate at all and was knocked to the ground. On getting up he turned to his assailants and quietly said, "Father forgive them for they know not what they do." This ended the incident for his assailants were also Christians and about to become ministers in churches.

To appreciate how radical Kagawa was let us consider this incident. To see people going to church dressed in expensive clothes shocked him. One Sunday he ran out in front of the churchgoers, blocked their path, and then began preaching: "Woe to you, scribes and Pharisees, hypocrites; for you are like whitewashed tombs, which outwardly appear beautiful, but within they are full of dead men's bones and all uncleanness. So you also outwardly appear righteous to men, but within you are full of hypocrisy and iniquity."

Kagawa began to be concerned about the poor and homeless. On the campus itself a beggar was living with his family in a shed without enough food.

He began wearing old clothes and one day the sister of one of the professors presented him with a brand new Japanese kimono. Kagawa thanked her very warmly but she noticed he never wore it. She presented him with another new one but again he did not wear it. What had happened was that he gave both to the children of the beggar's family. Kagawa was a rather unusual theological student; he believed in putting the teachings of Jesus into practice here and now.

When the war ended, Japan got Korea but had to withdraw from Manchuria. Some of the Japanese were very angry. A demonstration was held in the theatre near Kobe. A fight broke out and daggers were drawn, but suddenly Kagawa jumped on the platform and spoke: "Perhaps the terms of the treaty were wrong. But the people who rioted and set fire to the buildings in Tokyo were wrong too . . . When we think of the men we've lost and the millions of yen wasted, it's time we gave up our ideals of war." The audience applauded his remarks, and the fighting stopped.

Kagawa was so idealistic that he believed, "Our love must widen until it includes not only all humanity but created things as well." Kagawa gave himself so unselfishly for others that he came down with tubercular pneumonia. He decided to rent an old abandoned hut in a fishing village for fifty cents a month and went to live there. He spent his time writing a book, *Like a Dove,* but could not find a publisher. In the summer Dr. Myers came down to spend a few days with him in his one-room shanty. Kagawa was afraid he might catch his disease and warned him. Dr. Myers' answer was, "Man's love for his fellowman is even more contagious."

In the fall Kagawa returned to the Seminary and his studies. Because of the influence of one teacher, a popular professor was dismissed. Kagawa became a leader in urging the students not to attend the classes of the professor who had caused the trouble. Finally he and four others were expelled but Kagawa retorted to the President, "A school that teaches love should guide a mistaken student. God does not abandon us. Why should a seminary turn us out?"

Later when Dr. Myers came to plead with the President, all five students were taken back. Kagawa began preaching in the slums. The hungry children, the sick fathers and mothers, and the poverty and drunkenness preyed upon his mind. He decided to start working among the needy at once. Kagawa found a house in the slums with two rooms where a man had been killed and where everyone was afraid to live because his ghost was supposed to dwell there.

Kagawa took all his possessions and moved in. All around him were thieves, drunkards, ragpickers, garbage collectors, gamblers, street vendors and beggars. One beggar soon came to ask if he could share the house, then a bean curd seller who had killed a man for overturning his cart and had been sent to prison also asked for a place. Kagawa took them both in. Next he took in a man covered with the sores of some disease. Kagawa had ten yen a month from a job as a chimney sweep and eleven yen a month from his scholarship at the Seminary (ten and one-half dollars in all). But this was hardly enough to feed the four of them. Gangsters and beggars came, demanding money and clothes. Kagawa gave away one suit after another to those who were worse off than he. Finally all that remained were one cotton kimono and his school uniform.

The church began to contribute to his work. Dr. Myers helped all he could. Kagawa rented the three houses next to him, pulled down the partitions, and made one big hall, nine by thirty feet. Now he had a place for mission meetings and also a sleeping place for more of the penniless. He took in a beggar woman who was paralyzed and lived in a chicken coop with the hens. The doctor whom he called said her paralysis could be cured with proper care. A woman with five small children, deserted by her husband, was taken in. Soon the place was crowded to overflowing. He even took in an illegitimate baby from the jail where its mother was confined. This kept the others from sleeping but fortunately the mother took her back in four months time. When he had thirteen people in the home, an American began sending fifty dollars a month to help.

In 1913 Kagawa married a very devoted woman of his own age who had been helping in his work with the poor. In 1914 his manuscript, *Psychology of the Poor,* was accepted for publication. Kagawa decided to go to Princeton Theological Seminary in America and his wife would attend the theological Seminary in Yokohama. As he was sailing across the Pacific, World War I began.

In New York Kagawa found that the conditions in the slums resembled those in Japan. Wall Street and Fifth Avenue with its beautiful homes were not far from the squalor of the Bowery. He watched sixty thousand needle-workers who had lost their jobs because of the depression march by with banners reading: "We want bread." During the summer he was employed in the homes of the wealthy but twice he was fired, once because he had forgotten to lock the house properly. Nevertheless Kagawa succeeded in getting his B.D. degree from Princeton. But he had no money to get back home. In Ogden, Utah, he took a job as Japanese Association Secretary working in the beet fields and the copper mines. This gave him enough money to return to Japan. On reaching his native land he found he had trachoma, undoubtedly contracted while he was working in the slums. Soon his wife developed it also.

Fortunately his book which was published had a great success and the royalties began coming in. Thereafter he wrote constantly and had many books published. He organized a night school for laborers in Osaka and contributed some five thousand dollars from the royalties of his book to pay professors to teach there. At that time it was illegal to form a trade union in Japan. Kagawa believed this was against the teachings of Jesus. He organized the first dockworkers' union and became their leader. They went on strike for recognition and the right to negotiate. Their manifesto read in part: "Laborers are human beings. They are not to be bought and sold according to a scale of wages based on market prices. They are not machines." Kagawa pleaded for the use of nonviolence but some of the workers felt that they could never win this way. Kagawa's answer was, "They who take up the sword shall perish by the sword."

Eighteen thousand workers paraded down the street in support of the strike. In spite of all his pleadings one of the strikers threw a chunk of wood with nails into a window, breaking the glass. Kagawa and two hundred others were arrested and sent to prison. Fortunately he was sentenced for only thirteen days, and Kagawa found his prison cell far better than his home. It was a room, twelve by fourteen feet, and they even provided mosquito netting for the bed. After his release they had another peaceful parade and soon afterwards the dock owners met the union's demands. This was the beginning of unionism all over Japan.

Kagawa now began to organize peasant unions and schools for farmers. Suddenly his sight disappeared, and he was completely blind. But after two months of treatment in a hospital, his sight slowly returned.

On September 1, 1923 the greatest earthquake the country had ever known occurred in Yokohama. Kagawa and his wife organized relief for the homeless. They erected tents provided by the mission societies. About a thousand people slept in one of the Buddhist temples.

Kagawa's life was full and productive. Every morning he got up at five o'clock and spent an hour in meditation. Then he devoted the morning to writing books which would provide money for his work. He also traveled about the country giving talks and helping the people to organize for justice and peace. He helped establish nursery schools and kindergartens. He went abroad to lecture. Once he went to India and visited Gandhi and found himself in complete agreement with Gandhi's philosophy of love and nonviolence.

When he returned from one trip, Japan was beginning its invasion of China. He wrote a letter to China which was published in an American magazine and which read in part: "Forgive the sin Japan has committed upon you. The good people of Japan had no power or control over the militarists, but thoughtful men among them grieve over the sin of Japan." The result of this communication was posters all over Tokyo: *Kill the traitor Kagawa! He is against the nation! He is a traitor to the nation!* The next day, after preaching a sermon on nonviolence, Kagawa was arrested. He was released after eighteen days but fined for stating that a worker was as great as a king.

In 1940 during the war Kagawa was charged with subversive peace propaganda against the interests of the state and imprisoned again.

In 1941 Kagawa organized a week of prayer for a peaceful settlement of the Japanese-American talks. In spite of this, the bombing of Pearl Harbor took place. Posters began to appear: "Kill the traitor Kagawa!" He was attacked all over Japan. Although he had written some one hundred and thirteen books, no publisher dared to accept a manuscript from him now. A year after the outbreak of war Kagawa was arrested again but released after a few hours. When a young man refused military service and said he had been influenced by Kagawa, the noted Christian leader was brought to trial. This time he was ordered to keep silent for the duration of the war, and Kagawa agreed.

When Japan surrendered unconditionally, Kagawa came into his own. Japanese leaders now saw that he had been right. The Prime Minister of Japan asked him to become a counselor in his Cabinet, and he accepted. He also became Advisor to the Department of Welfare and persuaded General MacArthur to give food and lumber for shelters for those who had been left homeless as a result of the war. Kagawa became very popular and even gave a lecture to the Emperor and Empress in which he said, "Only through service to others can a man bring harmony and peace to the people."

In the 1930's when Kagawa came to the United States he was attacked by a group of Communists in San Francisco, and so the police across the country were alerted to protect him. He spoke in one of the rooms in Riverside Church in New York, and twenty policemen were on hand to see that there was no violence. Hardly had he begun to speak when one agitator after another jumped up to shout him down. The police began to take action to prevent these people from interfering, but Kagawa spoke up and pleaded with the police to leave the matter to him. When the police retired to the vestibule, then Kagawa with kindness, friendship and love in his words won the dissidents over, and the audience listened to his powerful and moving address. At the end the Japanese audience crowded around him with friendship and admiration in their hearts, including those who had tried to shout him down.

The author of this book knew Kagawa for a long, long time. In the twenties he had him speak to his classes in the Yale Divinity School. He visited Kagawa in his home in Tokyo. He put him on the Board of the Japan Religion and Labor Fellowship which he helped to start in Japan. Kagawa had long championed a world state and disarmament and wrote many published articles on these subjects.

We can all get inspiration from the life of Kagawa. He has now passed on to his reward. How will our own lives stack up against his? Think over some of his sayings: "Our love widens until it includes not only all humanity but created things as well." "God dwells among the lowliest of men. He sits on the dust heap among the prison convicts." "If we could learn to love one another it would be the solution to our problems."

If we can be moved by his life to devote our own to the service of humanity rather than to selfish gain and illusive happiness for ourselves, we would find the true happiness that comes from giving, not getting.

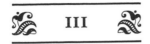

III

SIR WILFRED GRENFELL

I FIRST MET Dr. Wilfred Grenfell in 1915 when I was a student at Union Theological Seminary. I had heard of his magnificent work on the coast of Labrador and determined to spend the summer working with him. I had no money, but I volunteered to work as his secretary. He immediately accepted my offer but without compensation. This presented a problem. How was I to finance the trip? I decided to go down to Underwood & Underwood Company and offer to take pictures for them. They agreed eagerly, furnished all the needed photographic equipment, and arranged to pay me for the photographs they accepted.

The minute my classes were over I took a boat for St. Anthony, Labrador, and from there sailed with Doctor Grenfell on his hospital ship. I soon learned something of the background of the doctor.

He was born in Parkgate, England, on February 28, 1865. By 1889 he had secured his medical degree from Oxford University and was House Surgeon at the London Hospital where his father was Chaplain. In this work he visited outpatients in their own homes. One evening as he was coming back from such a call he heard singing in a large tent. Out of curiosity he went inside but became bored during a long prayer. He had started to walk out when the leader of the meeting called out "Let us sing a hymn while our brother finishes his prayer." Grenfell enjoyed singing and stayed on. The speaker was the famous evangelist, Dwight L. Moody, who challenged his hearers to follow Christ in their lives.

Grenfell decided to visit the tent meeting again a few days later, and this time two famous cricketers were speaking. At the close of their talks they called on everyone who was prepared to follow Christ in his life to stand up. Grenfell arose and from that time on sincerely tried to follow the Master throughout his life.

He first started a Sunday school class for the poor boys in the neighborhood which later led him to organize a summer camp for them at the seashore. This was very successful. London also had a mission for deep-sea fishermen which provided a doctor's services, and Grenfell was offered the job. He accepted with enthusiasm. Later on the mission decided to send a doctor to Labrador where the fishermen had no medical care. Grenfell was challenged by this opportunity and decided to go. He equipped a ketch-rigged schooner of under one hundred tons and had her hulls strengthened for cutting through ice. At twenty-seven years of age, on June 15, 1892, he left Yarmouth on this boat, the *Albert*. It took seventeen days to cross the Atlantic, and when it reached the city of St. Johns, Newfoundland, he found a fire raging which had destroyed churches, public buildings, and private homes. Many of the vessels in the harbor were burning. Grenfell immediately distributed clothes and blankets and cared for the injured. He soon found that nearly two hundred thousand of the population of Labrador were engaged in the fishing industry. He decided he must follow the fishing fleet which had just sailed for their summer fishing with thirty thousand men, women, and children on board. Early in August the *Albert* left St. Anthony for its four-hundred-mile cruise down the coast of Labrador. During this trip it had to avoid icebergs, rocks, and reefs.

When he reached Domino Run, which was a long, narrow creek, he had caught up with one hundred fishing boats. The fishermen were delighted when they learned he was a doctor and that he would not charge them for his services. He worked steadily treating cuts and minor ailments. Then he found there were people actually living on the shore, and in the first home he entered, a fisherman was dying of pneumonia.

In two months Grenfell treated over nine hundred cases. He was also called on to extract teeth and perform wedding ceremonies. When winter weather set in, Dr. Grenfell sailed south for he knew that the ocean would soon be frozen solidly. He had decided that he would have to establish a few hospitals staffed with doctors and trained nurses on the coast.

By the time the *Albert* reached St. Anthony, the news of Grenfell's work was all over the city. One merchant offered a place at Battle Harbour for a hospital; others raised money. One young man decided to go into medicine, and after nine years of study finished his work and joined the Mission.

Grenfell's success was so great that when he returned to England, the Mission Council decided to have him expand the work in Labrador. He left England on May 6th, 1893, and it was months later before Dr. Grenfell arrived at St. Johns. In the meantime he had treated over two thousand patients and made friends with Eskimos, fishermen, and natives. Several times he prevented whole families from dying from lack of food and clothing.

During the next winter Grenfell organized committees in Montreal, Ottawa, and Toronto, and money was raised for the Grenfell Mission. This enabled the Mission to have a fleet of four steamers the next summer. One of the boats was the *Sir Donald,* and Grenfell took it up to St. Anthony. Unfortunately, just as they were preparing to steam into the harbor with flags flying, they suddenly hit a submerged rock, and Dr. Grenfell and the others had to abandon ship. Luckily the vessel could be salvaged and repaired.

In May of 1915 when I went up to Labrador, Dr. Grenfell had a new hospital ship. It was the *Strathcona.* This boat burned wood instead of coal because patients often paid their fees in logs. She had six auxiliary sails also.

Below deck there was an operating room which was lighted only by a paraffin lamp; there were also bunks for those who were ill. We had a nurse and a graduate dentist from Harvard Dental School aboard. This hospital boat was small, only eighty feet long; consequently it rocked a great deal. The Harvard dentist left ship at the first port because he could not stand the motion and was seasick. Thereafter, I had to do the dental work or extraction, although my only training had been wielding a tennis racquet!

At every port the patients would swarm on board to be treated by the Doctor. If someone were too ill, we would go ashore to see him. If surgery was necessary, I might have to give the anaesthetic, since we had only one nurse.

During the course of the summer we were on fire once and ran aground three times; once we lost our anchor and once an iceberg crashed into us and deposited tons of ice on board. I could not even get into my cabin until we had split up the ice cakes and thrown them into the ocean.

I was surprised to find that many of the fishermen could not read or write so therefore patients did not necessarily follow directions. For example, a linament supposed to be used on an aching muscle might be swallowed to stop a stomach-ache. If a medicine was labeled *Take a teaspoon a day,* it might all be swallowed in a single day. Many of the people did not have enough to eat so there were cases of tuberculosis and scurvy. Sometimes both parents died, leaving the children in a dire predicament. Grenfell built a children's home in St. Anthony, and there orphan children were cared for. In some cases when the mother died and the father was left to care for four children, Dr. Grenfell arranged for some of the children to go to the home and gave clothing to the rest. Once a mother whose husband had died and who had six children gave him her twins who were partially blind. It was obvious that she could not care for all six children in the midst of the ice and snow of the far north. Thus, all along the way he responded to the needs of others and did a pioneering job.

Dr. Grenfell was also a magistrate. If a crime had been committed, he sometimes made arrests and tried the culprit on board ship. Once I was sent ashore to arrest a man who had committed rape. This assignment scared me a little, for I had to read the charges to the one who was to be arrested. Sure enough, when I reached his small home and knocked on the door, a great big six-foot-three fisherman with powerful muscles opened the door and said he was the man. After I had read the charges, he calmly put on his boots and quietly accompanied me to the dock and boarded the *Strathcona*. I acted as court stenographer and took down the proceedings of the trial. The man was duly convicted and placed on probation.

When I visited St. Anthony, I found that Grenfell had eighty in his children's home and two hundred pupils in the school which he had built there. When first brought in, the children were often without clothes and starving, but it was not long before they became strong again and completed their schoolwork satisfactorily. One of these boys became a store manager and another, a carpenter. One girl became a trained nurse.

Much to my surprise as we toured the coast in 1915, I found that Grenfell had established many hospitals, and we would visit each one.

At least seven thousand patients were treated in the hospitals alone, each year. Some of the people had beriberi because of the absence of fresh vegetables. Dr. Grenfell once brought down a herd of reindeer to get fresh milk for his hospital and for the children's home. This was all right while he had enough Laplanders to guard them, but when they went north again, poachers got busy stealing and killing the reindeer. In the end the Doctor had to give up this experiment.

I was deeply impressed by the devotion of his beautiful wife. I learned that he had been so busy that he had never married until he reached the age of forty-four. It happened that he was crossing the Atlantic to give some lectures and raise funds. On the *Mauretania* he met a banker, his wife, their daughter, and her friend Anne. Grenfell spent all his time with Anne. The ship took only a few days to cross the Atlantic, but before it docked in New York, he had determined to propose. At the time he didn't even know her last name, and her reply was "But you don't even know my name!" Quick as a flash Dr. Grenfell replied, "I don't care about what it is *now*, only what it is going to become." She invited him to visit her country home in Lake Forest, and they became engaged. They were married in November, 1909.

Mrs. Grenfell helped him raise money for his projects and worked with him effectively through the years. She was kindness itself to me. Whenever we landed in St. Anthony, I stayed at their home. I soon saw that they needed a new hospital, because the old one was not large enough to care for all of their patients. Twelve years after I was there, they dedicated a new hospital which was rated as first-class by the American College of Surgeons and which could take care of eight hundred patients each year.

I was fascinated, too, by the way that Dr. Grenfell met the economic problems of the fishermen. They usually sold their catch to merchants who toured the coast. They received far less than the prices in St. Anthony. At the same time the merchants charged them twice as much for food as they would pay in St. Anthony. Dr. Grenfell decided to break this situation by organizing cooperatives for the fishermen. They pooled their catch and shipped it down to St. Anthony where they got a high price. Then they bought their food jointly at wholesale prices. Of course this bitterly antagonized the owners of the merchant boats. They complained to St. Anthony, and the merchants there in turn complained to Canada, and their complaints in turn were sent to Grenfell's International Board in New York. Finally the Grenfell Board passed a resolution against the Doctor starting cooperatives in Labrador. They said that he had gone there to do medical and educational work and not to start cooperatives. Dr. Grenfell's reply was to submit his resignation. Because the Board realized this would be disastrous to the work, they rescinded their action. When I was with him, the cooperatives were operating successfully and were of inestimable value to the fishermen.

Dr. Grenfell was a very religious man. He held services on board his steamer and let me preach in the churches whenever we were in port on Sunday. He erected a church in St. Anthony, dedicated to St. Andrew, the fisherman of Galilee.

The time came when Grenfell was over seventy that he

had to retire because his doctors insisted that his heart was not up to the rigors of Labrador. On a trip around the world he became deeply interested in the desperate needs of the masses of Chinese people and expressed the wish that he had another life to give to serving them. He settled in Vermont near Lake Champlain. His wife died in 1939, and he followed her in 1940.

Wilfred Grenfell believed firmly in eternal life. He said that if a man were paralyzed from the neck down, there was only one fine nerve that permitted him to breathe and live. Dr. Grenfell could not believe that cutting this one nerve would mean that the man with all his character and highly developed mind was finished forever.

Naturally, in the light of his life, Dr. Grenfell demonstrated that to be a Christian meant living one's life in the service of others. He said, "When Christians merely preach sermons, the world sleeps." He was a great believer in prayer and daily devotions. He did not belong to one denomination, but said his church was of those "who do what Christ would do." His great services were recognized around the world. He held degrees from seven colleges and universities in the United States, from Toronto and McGill in Canada, and was knighted by King George V in 1927.

Each of us should give deep consideration to his life and work as contrasted with our own. Ponder these words of Dr. Grenfell: "Why is it that the very term 'religious life' has come to voice the popular idea that religion is altogether divorced from ordinary life? That conception is the exact opposite of Christ's teaching.

"To love one's neighbor as one's self is not a mere pious sentiment. It is every whit as much a law of life as fresh air is to the body."

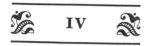

IV

JOHN R. MOTT

Dr. Mott was a courageous pioneer and builder of world Christian organizations. He was a leader whom God used to build Christian fellowship throughout the world. His life spans a large part of the history of the World Alliance of Y.M.C.A.'s.

I first met John R. Mott when he came to Oberlin in 1916, my second year of study in the Theological Seminary. World War I was on, and Dr. Mott wanted me to take my examinations at the beginning of April and go to Russia, then under the Tsar's regime, to work for the German and Austrian prisoners of war. He told me that modern weapons of war were so terrible that the conflict could not last through the summer so that I could be assured of getting back in the fall and not miss any of my work. I accepted his challenge, took my examinations, and fortunately asked each of my professors to give me a signed statement that I was to receive full credit for the year. The war continued until 1919, and when I came back, one of my professors said he could not have given me credit for the entire year when I took my examination in April. Fortunately, I had carefully saved his statement, and when I showed it to him, he smiled and said, "Bless my soul, I did not realize I was so kindhearted in those days."

Gradually over the years I came to learn more of Dr. Mott's background. He was born May 25, 1865, in Livingston Manor, New York. His father was in the lumber business, and the family moved to Postville, Iowa, in 1865. They were not very religious, but he was taught to say his prayers at night. It happened that J. W. Dean, Secretary of the State Y.M.C.A. and a devoted Christian and a Quaker, converted the boy's father who then joined the Methodist Church. The pastor of this church had a profound influence on the boy John and guided his reading. He also stimulated in him a desire to go to college.

At sixteen John R. Mott went to Upper Iowa University. There, he won prizes in debating and oratory, one of them on the subject, "The Chinese Should not be Prohibited from Immigrating to the United States of America." He decided to transfer to a larger school, Cornell University.

In the fall term of 1883, at a religious service for students conducted by Professor Colegrove, Mott arose and made a religious confession. After that he was a faithful member of the Sunday school and a charter member of the Y.M.C.A. In 1885, he began his work at Cornell and helped to raise the money for a Y.M.C.A. building on the campus. His religious life had been transformed at a meeting where the speaker emphasized, "Seekest thou great things for thyself? Seek them not. Seek ye first the Kingdom of God." Mott began by helping men in jail. He also spent an hour before breakfast studying the Bible. At this time he decided definitely to give his life to religious work and became President of the University Y.M.C.A.

In his last year at Cornell, he laid out a daily program which may even challenge the reader today!

Physical

Sleep—At least eight hours from 10 P.M. to 6 A.M. Go to bed to sleep, not to think.

Exercise—At least two hours in the open air, in the sun if possible.

Mental

University work—Review study schedule daily.

Aim to win. Study *vigorously* but not too many hours per day and take a little rest or change of position every hour.

Society—Have only a few intimates and those the best, for no man rises above the moral level of his intimates. Don't neglect the society of cultivated women.

Spiritual

Prayer—Study to improve on each preceding effort not only in the letter but in the spirit of prayer.

Bible—One-half hour per day pursuing some definite course.

Meditation—Set aside a few minutes (at least fifteen) every day for this purpose. Make out a self-examination chart and follow it.

Giving—Be systematic, and keep a private record of charities. Have at least one person's soul in view all the time. Under this heading be especially mindful of the poor, the neglected, the afflicted.

In 1887 Mott was offered by the librarian a chance to do a year's research with him abroad, with all expenses paid and to receive full credit for the year's work at Cornell. Mott turned down the offer, preferring to get the full benefit of his courses at Cornell. He was graduated in June, 1888, and immediately became National Secretary of the Intercollegiate Young Men's Christian Association of the United States and Canada. In the next few years he went back and forth across America, visiting and speaking to the students in the colleges and winning them to Christ. He also visited the preparatory schols and said, "If you capture the boys, they will become pillars for the work when they enter the colleges."

Mott also organized and spoke at student conferences on the Pacific Coast, at Northfield, Lake Geneva, and other centers. The present writer still remembers the Y.M.C.A. student conference he went to in the summer of 1912 when President of the Y.M.C.A. at Oberlin College. This was held at Silver Bay, N.Y., and Dr. Mott was one of the speakers. He gave a wonderful talk urging the students to follow Christ in their lives and made a profound impression on the delegates.

His work had already taken him on many round-the-world tours in which he visited some sixty-six countries. For instance, as early as 1894 Mott received invitations from Germany, Great Britain, Scandinavia and Switzerland to attend student conferences. In 1895 Mr. and Mrs. Mott took a world tour covering 60,000 miles, initiating student movements in India, China, Japan and Australasia.

In 1907 Dr. Mott organized the first student Christian meeting in Asia. The result was the organization of the World's Student Christian Federation. Dr. Mott stated his objectives in these words:

1. To unite student Christian movements throughout the world.
2. To collect information regarding the religious condition of students of all lands.
3. To promote the following lines of activity: (a) To lead students to become disciples of Jesus Christ as their Saviour; (b) To deepen the spiritual life of the students; (c) To enlist students in the work of extending the Kingdom of Christ throughout the world.

Once when Dr. Mott was riding in a Pullman train to Evanston in 1954, he had a conversation with the Negro porter about the forty countries around the world he had visited. Mott began to name them all. The porter showed interest, but in response to Mott's question as to whether he knew where they all were, came this quick reply, "Yes, sir, I'se been to all of them." Actually he had been in the Merchant Marine and had been around the world too. Mrs. Mott said she never saw John R. so "astonished and flattened out."

Dr. Mott says that when he is travelling by plane and wakes up in the morning he doesn't even know which country he is in, but he adds, "Whether it is South America, Finland, Japan, America, or France I know that Jesus Christ is there and has been preparing the way."

His first book was published in 1897, *Strategic Points in the World's Conquest*. Another book, which was somewhat optimistic, was *The Evangelization of the World in this Generation*, published in 1900. Altogether Dr. Mott wrote or edited eighteen books and forty-eight pamphlets. He also started a periodical, *The Student World*, and was its first editor.

He was Chairman of the World Missionary Council at Edinburgh in 1910 and was awarded the LL. D. degree by Edinburgh University.

Dr. Mott was heartsick at the mass slaughter and wounding of millions of men in World War I and he immediately started work for both the soldiers and the prisoners of war. By the second year of the war the cost of this program had risen to $800,000. At the peak of the war there were six million in the prison camps. The present writer was sent to Turkestan in Tsaristic Russia to serve the prisoners of war—German and Austrian. The conditions in the camps were appalling and the mortality rate staggering. This was checked by organizing the prison doctors, buying medicines for them, and increasing the food of the prisoners. Soon in one camp alone, 1200 prisoners were studying, using teachers who were themselves prisoners. Musical instruments were brought in and they soon had the finest orchestra in all Turkestan. A central Y.M.C.A. building and a library were set up; athletics and religious services for every faith were organized. I mention all this to show the incalculable benefits of the work inaugurated by Dr. Mott.

Later on the author started work among the Tsar's soldiers, because nothing was being done for them at all and ninety-two percent of them were illiterate. The Y.M.C.A. Club for the Russian soldiers duplicated the activities for the prisoners. Conditions were so frightful from a sanitary point of view in Turkestan that the author never ate anything unless it was cooked.

In a letter Dr. Mott wrote on May 2, 1916, he mentioned the fact that over 58 million men and boys around the world had already been forced into the armies, and nearly three million of them had been slain.

No wonder Dr. Mott felt that this far-flung work was of inestimable worth. In a letter, he used these words, "Against this black background of deadly strife and cruelty, of indescribable misery and suffering, the most inspiring and hopeful sight is our practical ministry on behalf of the millions of boys in the training camps, in the trenches, and in the prisoner-of-war camps.

In 1917 President Wilson asked Dr. Mott to go on a mission to Russia with Elihu Root. While in Russia he became convinced of the necessity of expanding the work in the Russian, French, and Italian armies and also in the terrible prisoner-of-war camps. Dr. Mott launched an appeal for money for this work and secured 55 million dollars. Later, seven organizations united and appealed for 170 million dollars. They actually raised over 200 million dollars.

Former President William H. Taft, later Chief Justice of the United States Supreme Court said of him, "There is no one of the present day who has a greater world vision of promoting the better side of all men and more experience fitting him to do so, than Dr. Mott. His knowledge of the moral and religious spirit of peoples of all countries and of the effective method of reaching and stimulating that part of their natures is extraordinary. Leaders in centers of influence the world over have a familiarity with his genius and capacity. This has made him a great agent in the process of civilization."

No wonder he received the Distinguished Service Medal from Secretary of War Newton Baker for the welfare services he rendered throughout World War I.

There are probably few leaders in the world who have done more to bring students to Christ than John R. Mott. He prepared for months before he came to a college by getting a small group in the school to enlist for planning, training classes, and prayer groups. He sent them books to strengthen their spiritual life and stimulate their zeal.

When Mott was holding meetings under the Tsar's regime in Moscow and St. Petersburg in 1909, he received the following two letters which in themselves spelled out the tyranny which brought on the Russian Revolution.

The letter of a woman student in Moscow:

> With great confusion I address myself to you, asking you to help me—to help me become clear in a question which torments me very much. For five years I have been engaged to a student. We could not marry till now for

the following reason: My mother is a very religious woman, she was badly disposed towards this student, has much wept, and fears his acquaintance because he is a revolutionist, and according to her opinion, he is an injury to our family, especially to my sister who has been put into prison, but has been delivered out of it and now is under observation of the police. Often Mamma, sobbing, addresses herself to the priest who is her confessor. Once he called me and said to me strongly, Leave him, otherwise you will be unhappy. Soon after that this priest died. I have struggled for a long time, I went to the war as a sister of charity, and this student wishing to smother his sorrow, began to work with energy in his party, and at last he was arrested and sent for five years to Siberia in a very retired place. He there languishes, already two years, and still must stay for three years. Teach me, Dr. Mott, where is the truth? I feel it is my moral duty not to leave this man who is deprived of everything.

A letter from a Jewish student:

You know, of course, through what hard experiences Russia has recently passed and is still passing. Take the newspapers — every day some execution. Are not "Christians" doing the hanging? Go in Moscow to the Butyrskaja Zastava; there you will see an immense prison. It is not pickpockets and robbers who are languishing there, but men who have committed no other crime than that of risking their own freedom for the freedom of the nation. But for the greatest part they are not Christians,—they fear the word "Christian." If they were free at present they would not go to hear your conference if they saw on the notice "Christian" Association. But are they not following Christ by their conduct? Do they not share His fate? Would not Christ Himself be thrown in prison with them if at present He should begin to

organize large meetings in order to fight against the official church as He did 2000 years ago in Palestine? It is
necessary in our country to re-estimate all values; everything with us is upside down.

After having read this letter please carefully destroy
my signature, because if by chance this letter with my
name should escape from your hands and should fall in
the hands of others . . . so it would be quite enough for
"Christians" to put its author into prison for an
indefinite time.

All around the world Dr. Mott spoke and the impact of
his message transformed the lives of thousands of students.
The reason for his success was his complete honesty and
truthfulness in reciting his facts, arguments, and experiences. He would also challenge his audience by confronting
them with the hardest test and the most painful fact,—the
demand made by God for the complete surrender of the
individual. He always held out hope to the individual
if he would show courage and take the path along the
way of Christ.

Dr. Mott felt that even more important than his speaking to students was recruiting leaders for the work. He said,
"I have given the greater part of my life to discovering,
enlisting, and selecting men, opening up avenues of opportunity for them, helping to train them, raising money to
support them." He believed that we must recruit them to
the personal discipleship of Christ and then to undertake a
specific task. In *The Future Leadership of the Church,* the
lives of 128 ministers were analyzed, including 100 leading
ministers of the past five centuries. He found that all except
nine came from homes which educated the child to give
his life to the Christian ministry. In this same book, he

analyzed the difficulties that prevent men from choosing the ministry:

"The materialistic spirit of the age, the temptation to make money, the power in the hands of industrial and financial magnates, parental ambition, the pleasure-seeking spirit of the times, the multiplication of lay-professions, the secular trend of education, the fear of restriction to oppose social injustice, civic corruption and ultra right-wingers, the pressure of young women with whom they associate, the fear of not being able to rise to the high moral and spiritual requirements of the ministry, seeing the inconsistencies and shortcomings of ministers and the impression that the ministry is lacking in spiritual and moral adventure."

Among the tests which Dr. Mott used in appraising a man he wanted for a task were:

1. Does he do little things well?
2. Has he learned the meaning of order as to time and place?
3. Does he understand priorities?
4. How does he use his leisure?
5. Has he intensity?
6. Does he take advantage of momentum?

Perhaps the greatest test is phrased in these words about leadership: "Our Lord said, 'He who would be greatest among you shall be the servant of all': leadership in the sense of rendering the maximum service; leadership in the sense of the largest unselfishness; in the sense of unwearying and unceasing absorption in the greatest work in the world, the building of the Kingdom of our Lord Jesus Christ."

Another field in which Dr. Mott was a master was the raising of funds for Christian work. It is probably true that during his life he was responsible for raising over 300 million dollars for Christian and philanthropic work. He did a great deal of this by seeing individuals directly and by raising money at his meetings. He always tried to get those who were planning meetings to take care to invite people of wealth to attend. When Mott began to work for the Foreign Department of the Y.M.C.A. of the United States and Canada in 1901, the budget amounted to some $50,000 and the foreign staff numbered only ten men. By 1928 the staff numbered two hundred and the budget was over 2 million dollars.

As early as 1910 Dr. Mott decided that the Y.M.C.A. should erect buildings in a score or more of cities around the world. He set up a goal of raising a million dollars for this purpose. He immediately went to Mr. Rockefeller and asked for half of this amount. Mr. Rockefeller sent Dr. Burton, later President of Chicago University, around the world to test the idea and when his report was received, decided to give the amount Mott had asked for. Dr. Mott then persuaded the President of the United States, Mr. Taft, to speak to a gathering of those who were going out to raise funds for the project, and Taft invited him to hold the meeting in the White House. The result was that eventually 2 million dollars was raised.

After World War I it was decided to go out for 5 million dollars for buildings. John D. Rockefeller, Jr., gave $1,250,000 and they actually raised over 6 million dollars. After the earthquake in Tokyo, Japan, Dr. Mott raised more than a million dollars for the Japan Rehabilitation Fund.

He believed that giving money was a test of spirituality. He said, "In soul-winning if you lead a soul that is *wandering,* that is lost, to the great Guide and Saviour, you do a work that will never die, because He is the same yesterday, today and forever. Just so, when we relate money to His Kingdom, which is an everlasting Kingdom, we have done work that will live after us through all generations."

He believed in raising money everywhere and in all places. As he said, "Money is all over the place, and you and I are responsible for discovering the money; we must follow the little rifts as they open; in the most unlikely places we are most likely to find the greatest things God has for us. Not long ago I was on a steamer the last place for finding a financial lead. But a certain man, a stranger, got into conversation with me. The conversation swung round till it led to his voluntarily offering me $5,000."

Dr. Mott believed in the world-wide rule of the Kingdom of God, and that money is just one instrument in bringing this about.

Naturally Dr. Mott was a great believer in World Peace. He felt this could be aided by building friendship between the youth of many nations rather than by the denunciation of war.

Ex-President Taft paid this tribute to Dr. Mott: "You are actually doing what the rest of us have been wishing and striving for. This great organization which you have developed is doing more than all the treaties or tribunals can accomplish, for you are leading the youth of these nations to cooperative effort, mutual trust, neighborly relations, and Christian love."

After the close of World War II the British Ambassador to Washington, Sir Cecil Spring Rice, wrote him: "You have done the most splendid work in secret. (Matt.VI:4) There is so much said about propaganda. I believe in deeds rather than words. . . . In this work you have played a most noble part and you have laid the foundation of true peace which is the mutual respect and affection of peoples."

In speaking to the World's Student Christian Federation in 1923 Dr. Mott recognized the appalling world in which we are living. He said, "It is in this mad world of class, international, and interracial strife with all its hideous consequences, that the members of our Federation are called to serve God and their fellowmen." Dr. Mott believed that the two principal blocks to peace were ignorance and wrong attitudes and that these could be changed by laying siege to the hearts and minds of youth. He felt that the world student movement with forty annual conferences and with hundreds of travelling secretaries was slowly weaving the fabric of friendship around the world. He believed that to build peace we need "an atmosphere of understanding in which men loathe to differ and determine to understand."

Dr. Mott did not swallow the easy words of bitter denunciation against the Communists. In the last months of World War I, he had this to say, "I resent many of the strictures placed upon Russia and many of the superficial, hasty, ill-considered judgments and criticisms concerning that vast and complex people and that wonderful nation. Already in this war the Russian people have laid away under the sod more than three million of their sons and brothers, their fathers and husbands, or more than all of the other Allies combined. When we have even 750,000 crosses over American graves in France, and perchance on other fronts, it may be fitting for us to criticize another nation for becoming tired of the war. Then I think of their two million men so maimed and mutilated that they can never fight again . . . Do you wonder that the Russians are war-tired?"

Dr. Mott also served on a commission appointed by the President to settle Mexican differences. He became a real peacemaker and the Director of Primary Education in Mexico City wrote him: "I am absolutely sure that you will be an instrument in the hands of God to settle these troubles and secure permanent and firm friendship between our two nations."

Dr. Mott also believed in interracial equality and friendship and did everything he could in the Southern states to promote this.

The writer saw Dr. Mott in Florida not long before his death. We were entertained at the home of Col. Raymond Robins. In the middle of the luncheon Dr. John R. Mott then eighty-four years of age leaned over and said, "Dr. Davis if you and I live to be very old men we will never have a better luncheon than this."

Here is the three-fold touchstone which Dr. Mott used in his life:

1. Genuine, unflinching allegiance to Jesus Christ.
2. The creative strength of group fellowship in thought and prayer and action.
3. International interdependence of movements around the world and continuing new leadership with courage and new ideas.

Mott had vision, daring, and the ability to think in world terms. Do we who are reading these words share his consecration and outlook?

Today the World Alliance of Y.M.C.A.'s has a world headquarters at Geneva, Switzerland, called the John R. Mott House in dedication to his memory.

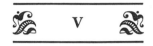

V

VLADIMIR ILYICH LENIN

How do we deal with a world which believes that the answer to the threat of communism is massive military power? This is the doctrine of peace through deterrance. In all human history this policy has never succeeded. If two sides arms to the teeth, in due course war eventuates.

I was sent to Russia under the Tsar's regime forty-seven years ago to work for the American Y.M.C.A. serving the prisoners of war in Turkestan. In the first camp when I began my work, seventy-five were dying every day, and I supervised twenty-five camps. I had the Tsar's secret service on my trail twenty-four hours a day. They even slept in the same house where I stayed. No letters ever reached me through the mail. I had to pick them up from the Tsar's censor. I could not mail any letters but similarly had to take them to the censor. Ninety-two percent of the people were illiterate, and there were no doctors in the rural areas.

I realized that these conditions must be changed, but how? I believed that if the starvation, the disease, and the illiteracy were not eliminated by peaceful means, then violence would result. It did, and Kerensky came into power.

He inaugurated some changes, but the devastating World War I continued. This meant that money, time, and effort could not be used to eliminate the dreadful conditions of the Russian people. I began to feel that unless the war ended, violence would again result, and it did.

When I was working for the American Y.M.C.A. in charge of clubs for the Russian soldiers, I first heard of Lenin. I was told he "was a dangerous man who wanted to seize the power by violence." I first saw Vladimir Ilyich Lenin when he arrived in St. Petersburg on April 16, 1917. He had secured permission from the German government to go through in a sealed car from Switzerland. Undoubtedly, the Kaiser hoped he would foment a revolution in Russia and thus make it easier for Germany to conquer and defeat her.

I was eager to see Lenin and was at the Finland Station to see the demonstration. The station square and all the nearby streets were jammed with people. As he came out of the railway station, Lenin climbed on top of an armored car and began congratulating the workers on having freed Russia from the autocracy. He ended his remarks by saying, "Long live the Socialist Revolution." I was quite impressed with Lenin's appearance. He looked young and vigorous. He seemed to be absolutely sincere and to want to do everything to help the people. I began to investigate his background.

Lenin's father, Ilya Ulianov, was born in Astrakhan into a poor family. His father died when Ilya was only seven. Ilya Ulianov's whole career was made possible by the devotion of a brother who abandoned all dreams of education to spend his whole life working for his mother, two sisters, and younger brother. He never even married. The brother furnished the funds that enabled Ilya, Lenin's father, to go through the *gymnasium* and then through Kazan University to become a teacher of mathematics and physics.

At that time the majority of the population were virtually slaves whom the landlords could flog, sell like cattle,
marry off at will, or exile to Siberia. There were revolutionists in those days, but most of them either died on
the gallows or were subjected to a lingering death in penal
servitude.

After the death of Tsar Nicholas, Alexander II abolished
serfdom so as to make more workers available for capitalist industry. Ilya, Lenin's father, was offered the post of
Inspector of Elementary Schools in Simbirsk which he
accepted. During the seventeen years of his tenure, the
number of schools increased to four hundred and fifty in
the district. He worked so hard that in his fifty-fifth year he
suffered a fatal cerebral hemorrhage.

Vladimir Ilyich Ulianov (or Lenin, as he was later
called) was born on April 22, 1870, in the town of Simbirsk
on the banks of the Volga River. His mother was well
educated and conversant with several foreign languages.
At five years of age Lenin had learned to read. At the age
of nine and a half he entered the first form of the *gymnasium*. He was at the head of his class every year, receiv-
ing the annual first prize plus a certificate and a book with
these words stamped in gold: "For Good Conduct and
Progress." Part of his scholastic success was due to personal tutoring by his father. One of his reports read:
"Punctuality: perfect. Preparation of lessons: perfect.
Attention: perfect. Written exercise: very assiduous. Interest in study: very great, especially for ancient languages."

The father of Kerensky was the principal of the high
school from which Lenin graduated. He made this written note in his records: "Very gifted, always punctual and
diligent, Ulianov was first in all the classes and received
a gold medal upon the conclusion of his studies as the

most deserving of all the students in progress, development, and conduct."

Vladimir had an excellent memory, was conscientious about all of his work, and always read a great deal, constantly borrowing books from the library. Ever willing to help his classmates with the difficult assignments in Greek and Latin, in his last two years in the *gymnasium* he even coached a teacher for the examination that would enable him to enter the university; all of this help was given gratis. Lenin helped one boy cover an eight-year course in Latin in two years. When at the outset the boy expressed doubt that this would be possible, Lenin replied, "In school, naturally, with their stupid system of teaching, they have to spend eight years on the Latin course, but a grown-up rational human being can easily cover it in two years."

When Lenin was about fourteen years of age, a neighbor asked his father whether his children attended church regularly. The father said, "No," and then sent young Lenin away on an errand. When he returned, the visitor smiled and said, "Give him the stick; don't spare it." This angered Lenin, and he ran out into the garden, removed the cross he was wearing, and threw it away. There were so many superstitious practices in the Russian Orthodox Church that it did not take much to convince Lenin that it was all "fictitious delusion."

When Lenin was sixteen, his father died. A year later his elder brother, Alexander, was arrested for participating in an attempt to kill Tsar Alexander III. He was tried, convicted, and on May 8, 1887, executed. This undoubtedly had a profound effect on Lenin and influenced him to devote his life to the Revolution. In court, his brother Alexander had admitted to having left the university in order to end forever the despotism and lack of freedom that prevailed in the country. He even confessed that he had made bombs with which to kill the Tsar. Lenin was convinced that assassination of government officials was not the way in which to remedy injustice and said, "No, we will not take that path."

This same year Lenin finished the *gymnasium* and was awarded a gold medal for his scholastic work. He was admitted to the law school of Kazan University, and his mother moved to this town, taking the whole family with her. At this time the Tsar's government was especially harsh on students, subjecting them to searches, arrests and sentences of exile. The government used such methods as surveillance and spying, dismissal of the more liberal professors, prohibition of all organizations, and expulsion of anyone compromised in the eyes of the authorities.

On December 4, 1887, the students of Kazan met together and demanded to see the Inspector. When he appeared they put forth demands for more freedom in the university. Lenin was one of the leaders at the meeting. He was arrested that same night and spent several days in jail at the police station. The police officer who took Lenin into custody said to him, "What's the use of rebelling, young man? Don't you see that there's a wall before you?" Lenin replied, "Yes, but the wall is thoroughly rotten. Give it a good push, and it will topple over."

Lenin was expelled from the university and sent to the village of Kokushkino, twenty-six miles from Kazan, where his sister was living under house arrest. Her original sentence of five years in Siberia had been amended to allow her to move there. The mother and the rest of the family soon went there too.

Vladimir Ilyich was now able to do a lot of reading.

He had the books and magazines belonging to his uncle and could also get books from the Kazan library.

To show how dangerous his environment was, Lenin once wrote a letter to a fellow student who had entered another university in the south, describing what had happened to him. His sister finally persuaded him not to send it, as it might get the other student into trouble.

In the fall of 1888, Lenin received permission to live in Kazan, and the family moved back there. It was here that he began to study the first volume of Marx's, *Das Kapital.* Lenin was very enthusiastic and optimistic about Marx's theories. He believed that the path Marx had shown was the only practical road to socialism. He met with revolutionary-minded students every now and then to talk things over. They did not come to his house, since it was under police observation, but Lenin would meet with them.

Lenin now began to smoke, which disturbed his mother who was afraid of the harmful effects of tobacco. She used every argument she knew, pointing out the dangers of the habit. Finally she said, "We cannot afford to incur the extra expense of smoking, however small, for we are all living on my pension." This clinched the matter with Lenin, and he gave up smoking, never to return to it for the rest of his life.

Vladimir Ilyich made repeated attempts to re-enter the university but was always refused. Finally, the authorities said he could take his examinations, and in 1891, he took his degree at Petersburg University. He had mastered the entire four-year course in a year and a half. In 1892, he began to practice law, but this was only to disguise his revolutionary activities. He read intensively, and since he knew foreign languages, he was able to get books from the library which most Russians could not use. He continued his studies in Marx and Engels, becoming more and more convinced that they were right. He stayed in Samara for three years during which time he met regularly with radical groups such as the Narodniks and the Narodnaya Volya. He committed to memory their methods of revolutionary struggle, conspiratorial stratagems and prison conditions, and how to make contacts with the outside world while in confinement.

In 1893, Vladimir Ilyich went to St. Petersburg to begin his revolutionary activity. There he formed an organization called "The League of Struggle for the Freedom of the Working Class." He looked for people who shared his views that revolution in Russia would be the result of action by the working people or not happen at all. He was therefore opposed to the Legal Marxists and the Economists who denied the necessity of political struggle by the workers and were inclined to work through the peasants.

Lenin spent a great deal of time in the workingmen's section of the city, devoting his efforts to educating the workers. He wrote many pamphlets championing the Social Democrats and portraying the exploitation of the workers. In 1894 he wrote a pamphlet entitled, *Who Are the Real Friends of the People?* In this he outlined his belief that when the workers were organized and educated, they would overthrow the autocracy and usher in "the victorious communist revolution." When he went abroad he had a suitcase made with a false bottom, which enabled him to bring back illegal literature.

By September, 1895, Lenin found that he was being shadowed continuously. He had to become an expert in throwing off the police sleuths. Sometimes while being followed he would dash into a slum apartment house, hide in a closet, and watch his pursuer running about hope-lessly. Of course, since Lenin was going to secret meetings, visiting workers in their homes, distributing illegal liter-ature, and printing leaflets of his own, the police eventu-ally caught up with him. On December 9, 1895, Lenin was arrested. The conditions of the cells in the municipal jail in which he was confined were awful in comparison to other prisons he had been in. Lenin said, "Vermin give me no peace day or night. The filth is intolerable, and every night we have to endure the noise and swearing of police-men and spies who play cards near the cells."

He decided to use his time in prison by writing a book which would be called, *The Development of Capitalism in Russia*. Fortunately, books were allowed rather freely in the prison, and he could even get them from the public library.

The League for the Struggle for the Freedom of the Working Class had now become very popular. While Lenin was in prison, the factory workers asked for pamphlets. So Lenin began to write illegal pamphlets. He wrote in milk between the lines of books; when heated, this writing would show up. In his cell he made "inkpots" of bread, and if a guard came to look at him through the spyhole, he would pop the "inkpot" into his mouth. Lenin said that one day he had to swallow six "inkpots" because the guards were spying. When he got these books out to his sister, she would copy out his secret writing after heating the pages against a lamp. Then she would destroy the original and hide her copy in a hollow table leg.

In 1897, Vladimir Ilyich received a three-year sentence to Siberia. While he was in exile, the First Congress of the Social Democratic Party named him to be editor of the party paper and commissioned him to write its program. Also, while in exile he married his fiance, Nadezhde Konstantinova Krupskaya. He finished his book *The Development of Capitalism in Russia* there. Actually, he wrote thirty books and pamphlets while in Siberia.

When Lenin was finally released, he decided that it would be impossible to hold the Second Party Congress inside Russia. Instead he determined to go abroad and edit a Russian newspaper. He went to Munich in Bavaria and there began to publish a paper called *Iskra* (The Spark) which had as its motto, "The spark will kindle a flame." It was sent into Russia for secret distribution. The message which it reiterated was that the only practical program was the overthrow of the Tsar's regime and the establishment of a democratic republic.

While Vladimir Ilyich was in Siberia, his younger brother Dmitry had been arrested as well as his sister Maria. Shortly after Lenin's return he was again arrested but this time released. He escaped by crossing the Gulf of Finland at night and almost lost his life when the ice gave way, but he did get abroad.

Lenin had perfected the techniques of an agitator. I heard him speak at mass gatherings. I read his appeals to workers through the press. Lenin believed that the usual methods of agitation were not enough. He wrote: "Agitation should be carried on among Red Army men by workers singly or in groups, in barracks, Red Army units and factories. . . . The trade unions must institute a check to see that every one of their members takes part in house-to-house agitation, distribution of leaflets, and personal talks."

In fact, he maintained close and constant contact with the masses. His secretary said: "Lenin was always able to put heart into the working people with his own unshakable faith in the victory of the people's cause, to encourage them with ardent, compelling and infinitely truthful words, to point out to the masses ways and means of overcoming the difficulties, and define not only the immediate practical aim of the struggle but also unfold before them the great prospects of building a new society . . . he had iron-clad logic, deep conviction, and unshakable faith in the rightfulness of the cause he championed."

In 1903, Lenin wrote a pamphlet entitled *To the Rural Poor*. This was an appeal to the peasants to join with the workers. It said: "We want to achieve a new and better order of society. In this new and better society there must be neither rich nor poor; all will have to work. Not a handful of rich people, but all the working people must enjoy the fruits of common labor. Machines and other improvements must serve to ease the work of all and not to enable a few to grow rich at the expense of millions and tens of millions of people." To achieve this goal Lenin believed in the dictatorship of the proletariat. He believed that all members of the Communist party must submit to its discipline, but the party should be open to all who agreed with its program, paid their dues, and took an active part in its work.

One of Lenin's favorite spots was a library—any library. He was a frequent visitor to libraries abroad. He worked in the Imperial Library in Berlin, in the National Library in Paris, at the British Museum in London, and in Geneva, he had to make application to use the library and pay a small fee. He always felt it was wrong to take isolated facts and derive a case from them; instead he said we must take "the sum total of facts bearing on the problem under discussion."

In 1902, when he was thirty-two, he gave a series of

lectures at the Institute for Social Sciences in Paris. Professor Kovalevsky remarked afterwards, "What a fine professor Lenin could become!" But Lenin felt he could accomplish far more through revolutionary activity. In an article, "What Is To Be Done?" he wrote that trade unionism alone cannot save the workers. "The workingmen can be saved only by an organization of revolutionaries which, unlike the labor units, must consist exclusively of people whose profession is revolutionary activity. Such an organization must not be too wide and must be as secret as possible."

Lenin tried to win the majority of the members of the Russian Social Democratic party to his views. At the convention in 1903, he won a majority, and hence his faction was named the Bolsheviki (majority). In 1904, however, the Menshiviki (minority) obtained the majority. As a result Lenin founded the Bolshevik paper *Forward,* editing it in Switzerland.

After the Russo-Japanese war in 1905, Lenin returned to Russia on a forged British passport and lived in Petrograd under an English disguise. He started a newspaper with the poet Minsky as one of the editors. Lenin was genial and modest but had an iron perseverance in all matters affecting the party. Kinsky wrote of him, "Those who knew Lenin well twenty years ago never doubted that sooner or later he would play the first role in the history of his country. There was a legendary heroic halo round Lenin's personality."

At the Congress of the Russian Social Democrats in 1907, Lenin argued that in a revolution not only must the aristocracy be overthrown but capitalism as well. He said, "He who storms a fortress cannot give up fighting after taking the fortress. Either we take the fortress to hold it or we need not storm it."

At the International Socialist Congress in Stuttgart, Lenin urged that in the event of a war the Socialist parties turn it into a war against the capitalist system.

From 1908 to 1911, Lenin lived in Paris. At this time the Tsar in Russia was sending hundreds of thousands of revolutionists to prison in Siberia, and any opposition was being suppressed with death. In a private letter, Lenin wrote, "The times are as difficult as hell."

When World War I broke out, Lenin was living in Poronino. From the very first days of the war Lenin was bitterly opposed to it. He began telling the workers, "Turn the imperialist war into a civil war."

One of the problems Lenin faced abroad was that of earning a living, and he frequently had to write articles to produce an income.

During World War I, Lenin settled in Zurich. He took part in the Zimmerwald Conference in 1915 of anti-war socialists. The total financial resources of the Conference were only fifty francs, and its first publication resulted in a deficit of fifty francs. Lenin attacked the German socialist leaders for their support of the Kaiser.

While I differed with Lenin in his faith in the materialistic philosophy of Karl Marx and in the dictatorship of the Communist party, I agreed with Abramovitch, the famous Menshevist leader who, although in opposition to Lenin, wrote, "It would be mistaken to imagine Lenin as a demoniacal being. On the contrary, his home life and personal relations would merit the enthusiasm of any Baptist minister. It is difficult to conceive a simpler, kinder, and more unpretentious person than Lenin at home."

When he returned to Russia, the Provincial Government was in power. On July 5th the offices of *Pravda,* the newspaper Lenin edited, were raided. Lenin feared they would raid his home so he departed; it was raided that night, and thoroughly searched. Lenin fled, eventually hiding in Finland and taking refuge in the home of the chief of police in Helsingfors who was a communist.

Lenin believed: "The transformation of the war into a civil war is the one good watchword for the working class."

A month after Lenin's return to Russia, the first national conference of the Bolshevik party took place, and Lenin's proposals were adopted in their entirety. He now became the ruling power in the party.

In the middle of October Lenin addressed a letter to the Bolshevik organizations in Moscow and Leningrad in which he said:

Dear Comrades:

Events are dictating our task to us so clearly that delay is becoming positively a crime.

The agrarian movement is spreading. The Finnish troops and navy are against the government.

It is clear that a revolution is beginning in Germany, especially after the executions of the sailors. The elections in Moscow, returning 47 percent Bolsheviks, are a gigantic victory. With the Left Socialist-Revolutionists we have an obvious majority in the country.

The railroad and post office workers are in conflict with the government. The Libers and Dans, instead of a Congress meeting on the 20th of October, are already talking of a Congress 'in the twenties.'

In such circumstances waiting is a crime.

Bolsheviks have no right to wait for the Congress of Soviets. They must seize power at once. They would save thereby the world revolution. . . .

To delay is a crime. To wait for the Congress of Soviets

is an infantile play in formalities, a shameful game, a betrayal of the revolution. If power cannot be taken without an uprising, then we must go in for an uprising at once.

On the night of October 10th, a meeting of the general staff of the Bolsheviks took place which was to plan the uprising, with Lenin, Trotsky and Stalin in attendance among others. The day for the revolt was set for October 17, 1917. The Provisional Government had declared Lenin an outlaw, issued a warrant for his arrest, and probably would have been glad if he could have been assassinated.

I gradually began to have doubts as to whether the Kerensky Government could remain in power unless they did more for the peasants and more for peace.

On the day the Bolsheviks seized power in St. Petersburg, I had an appointment with Kerensky in the Winter Palace. Among the questions I asked was whether there was any danger of the Bolsheviks seizing the power. Kerensky laughed and with a wave of his hand said, "Not the slightest danger in the world." That night he was fleeing for his life, and the Bolsheviks took over as Lenin had predicted. I returned to Moscow and helped to carry in the dead and wounded as an American Y.M.C.A. worker. As I expected, the Bolsheviks won the power.

On the evening of October 25th (November 7th) the Second Congress of Soviets opened in Smolensk. It had six hundred and fifty delegates with over four hundred Bolsheviks. It voted that all power now resided in the Soviets. A decree on peace was passed stating, "War is the greatest crime against humanity."

Before long the Bolsheviks made peace with Germany although they would not have done this if the United States had been willing to help them in the fight.

By this time the United States, England, France, and Japan decided to intervene and overthrow the Bolsheviks. All our American Y.M.C.A. secretaries were withdrawn from communist Russia and placed behind the United States troops. The American ambassador said Lenin and Trotsky would be arrested or killed within two months. I did not believe this would happen and returned to the United States to speak against the intervention. My prediction proved accurate, and the Bolsheviks won the power throughout Russia.

I heard Lenin speak several times. He was very modest, although his audiences gave him great ovations. He would often say, "You are cheering the Revolution, not me."

Lenin was most generous in being available to people. While I was in charge of all the American Y.M.C.A. war work I saw him a number of times. When I asked for it, he even gave me his autograph on a picture of himself. He lived very simply, wore inexpensive clothes, and was satisfied with the barest necessities. Once he said that the communists would train all the children in Russia to read and then "The seed I have sown will never be uprooted." He had always believed the Provisional Government could not be trusted and that all power must be in the hands of the Soviets.

Lenin's life was always in danger. On January 1, 1918, as he was driving back to his headquarters, his automobile was riddled with bullets. On this occasion, Lenin threw himself on the floor and was not hurt.

On August 30, 1918, M. I. Uritsky, Chairman of the Petrograd Cheka, was assassinated. Shortly afterwards in Moscow, Fanny Kaplan, a terrorist, shot at Lenin just after he had spoken in a factory. She was under orders to do this from the Central Committee of the Party of Right

Socialist-Revolutionists. She fired three shots—two bullets wounded Lenin and the third tore his coat in the back. It was later discovered that he was wounded with explosive, poisoned bullets, but for some reason the bullets did not explode.

His secretary said: "But even in his suffering Lenin displayed the matchless greatness of his spirit. He went on thinking of the future of his country, of the cause which he had served selflessly all his life. Lenin's bonds with the working masses were strong and unbreakable. Even when he was gravely ill, he was entirely with the people in thought."

While he recovered from this attack, Lenin was never well again, and in 1924 he died.

One of my close friends in Russia was Col. Raymond Robins, head of the American Red Cross. He saw Lenin constantly and in one of their many conversations Lenin said: "The American government is living in the *political* thinking of a bygone *political* age. It is living in the age of Thomas Jefferson. It is not living in the present *economic age*. Therefore, it is lacking in intellectual integrity. How shall I make it clear to you? Well, consider this:

"Consider your states of New York and Pennsylvania. New York is the center of your banking system. Pennsylvania is the center of your steel industry. Those are two of your most important things—banking and steel. They are the base of your life. They make you what you are. Now if you really believe in your banking system and respect it, why don't you send Mr. Morgan to your United States Senate? And if you really believe in your steel industry, in its present organization, why don't you send Mr. Schwab to the Senate? Why do you send men who know less about banking and less about steel and who protect the bankers and the steel manufacturers and pretend to be independent of them? It is inefficient. It is insincere. That is why I say that your system is lacking in integrity. That is why our system is superior. That is why it will destroy yours.

"Our system will destroy yours because it will consist of a social control which recognizes the basic fact of modern life. It recognizes that real power today is *economic* and that the social control of today must therefore be *economic* also. So what do we do? Who will be our representative in our national legislature, in our national Soviet from the district of Baku for instance?

"The district of Baku is oil. Oil makes Baku. Oil rules Baku. Our representatives from Baku will be elected by the oil industry. They will be elected by the workers in the oil industry.

"You will say that your republic is a *citizens'* republic. Very well. I say that man as a producer is more important than man as a citizen. The most important citizens in your oil districts—who are they? Are they not the oil men? We will represent Baku as oil.

"The representatives from the Donetz Basin will be representatives of the coal industry. Again, from the country districts, our representatives will be representatives chosen by peasants who grow crops. What is the real interest of the country districts? It is not storekeeping. It is not money-lending. It is agriculture . . . .

"This system is stronger than yours because it admits reality. It seeks out the sources of daily human work-value and, out of these sources directly, it creates the social control of the state. Our government will be an *economic* social control for an *economic* age. It will triumph because it speaks the spirit and releases and uses the spirit of the age that now is . . . .

"Colonel Robins, you do not believe it. I have to wait for events to convince you. You may see foreign bayonets parading across Russia. You may see the Soviets and all the leaders of the Soviets killed. You may see Russia dark again as it was dark before. But the lightning out of that darkness has destroyed political democracy everywhere. It has destroyed it not by physically striking it, but simply by one flash of revealment of the future."[1]

Later Robins said, "This man Lenin is a great man. These people will go the limit for him. Anyone who thinks leadership like that can be beaten by what we see of the opposition in Russia is crazy."

How then shall we appraise a leader like Lenin? This is a most difficult task, but today, in the light of half a century, we can at least try to evaluate his character. By the time he was twenty-three Lenin accepted the faith of Marxism and gave everything he had to its realization. He had a penetrating mind and a dedicated devotion to what he believed to be true. He desired nothing for himself; he was unselfish to a fault. He was ascetic in his habits and extremely modest in his contact with other people, but he was resolute and unshakable in the pursuit of what he believed to be in the interests of all the people.

Lenin was determined to establish a social and economic order which was for the benefit of all the workers, both peasants and farmers. He was born and grew up under one of the worst dictatorships of his era, the Tsar's tyranny. He was a champion of the ignorant, toiling masses and he realized that they needed leadership.

[1] See William Hard, *Raymond Robins' Own Story*. (New York, Harper and Brothers, 1920) , pp. 159-163.

He accepted the principle that there must be a just and equitable distribution of all the wealth in the world, and he believed that this was impossible under capitalism.

He was a man of action. Once he believed that a course of action was right, he gave to it everything he had.

Lenin always tried to act so as to attain the goal in which he believed. Under the Tsar, he saw nothing possible except armed revolution. When the Germans were advancing into Russia after the revolution had occurred, he rightly saw that the Soviet armies would be unable to stop them. Against the opinion of many of his colleagues he urged the acceptance of the Brest-Litovsk Peace Treaty instead of trying to wage a war against capitalist Germany without help from the West.

History has also shown that Lenin was probably right in the long run in believing that it was the industrial workers that the revolutionary forces would have to rely on. This is true, even if in Red China with its huge peasant population, for the time being the peasantry is overwhelmingly important. Lenin, too, was willing to make concessions to the peasants as he did in his New Economic Policy in 1921. Lenin also saw clearly the corroding veneer of materialism on the Hebrew-Christian ideology as is too often the case.

Each reader should ask himself, "What are the lessons that I can learn for my own life from that of Lenin? Do I have his dedication? Do I give everything I have to the causes in which I believe as he did? Is my life devoted to helping the masses of the world to secure justice and happiness?"

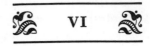
COLONEL RAYMOND ROBINS

RAYMOND ROBINS was one of the most colorful, dynamic, and unusual men I have ever met. I had known him off and on ever since the revolutionary days in Russia when he was the head of the American Red Cross there. At that time he invited me to become his assistant, but I declined, feeling I ought to remain with the American Y.M.C.A. war work in Russia.

He was born in 1873 on Staten Island but spent his boyhood years in Zanesville, Ohio, in Louisville, Kentucky, and in Florida. His father was a private banker. At the age of ten the boy was sent to Florida to live with his cousin. The cousin lived in an undeveloped area in Florida. He had started an orange grove and had hired a Negro named Fielder Harris, who could neither read nor write, to help him. Fielder became the companion of Raymond, taught him the habits of birds and animals, and all his life Robins had a great affection for him. For the seven years that Raymond was there he milked the cows, helped in the fields, and became the close friend of Fielder. But at seventeen years of age and with about eighteen dollars which had been given him in tips and gifts, Raymond decided to go out and earn money and become rich.

He started with the job of deputy postmaster at Istachatta. After suffering from malaria for some months, he went to Ocala and got a job at $40 a month in a hardware store. However, he found he could barely live on this amount and took a job in a coal mine in Tennessee where he received a dollar a day plus room and board, such as it was. The miners lived in tents with bunks six tiers high, and they worked twelve hours a day. In those days there were no workmen's compensation laws, and the families of the miners who were killed in a cave-in received nothing. Robins learned from a fellow worker about the trade union movement and began organizing the men. When they had enough members in the union, they asked the mine superintendent to give them an eleven-and-one-half-hour day and $1.10 an hour for labor, with a half day off each week. The only response they received was "Get the hell out of here." A strike resulted, with the militia killing some of the strikers. After it was over, Robins was barred from any job in the town. He hitchhiked his way out to Leadville, Colorado, and got a job in a union mine at $3.60 for eight hours and a six-day work week. He thus experienced at first hand the benefits of union organization. After saving his money on this job, he decided to go out as a prospector to win a fortune.

First, he studied law in San Francisco and also campaigned for William Jennings Bryan for the presidency in 1896. Then in August, 1897, he sailed out of the Golden Gate for the far north and Alaska.

He figured that if he failed in his prospecting he would sell out to the political machines and get a good job. After he arrived, it took him twenty-six days to go forty miles up the canyon, over rocks, frozen rivers, and snow drifts to the Chilcoot Pass. At this time he was smoking two packs of cigarettes a day but decided that if he was going to succeed in getting through the ice and snow, he would have to give up every handicap. So he sold his unused cigarettes and then gave up liquor. He also stopped gambling.

Eventually he made a thousand miles over the snow and decided to camp at Mountain Village for the winter. However, there were four in the party, and they did not have enough food so Robins and a man named Puckett decided to go on.

On their way, they joined another group. Robins was impressed by one man in the party who would always help anyone who fell into a crevice and who would go out of his way to bring cheer to everyone. He never lost his temper no matter what happened, as Robins sometimes did. At night Robins found this man reading his New Testament before he went to sleep. Robins asked, "Why don't you ever lose your temper as we all do?" The man replied, "I suppose it's because I am a Christian." Robins retorted, "Oh, hell, that doesn't mean anything, what's the real reason?" Instantly, the answer came, "It means something if you're a *real* Christian," and this made Robins think.

Robins said: "I wiped the church out of my life for nearly eighteen years and never went to church or had anything to do with religion in that time." He believed a preacher was "a good enough sort of guy, drawing down more money for less work at that job than any other."

The group finally reached the Roman Catholic mission at Kosserevski, the most northerly mission in the world. Robins was opposed to the Catholic Church, but here they were entertained hospitably. The temperature outside was fifty degrees below zero.

Father Barnum invited Robins to look the mission over with him. He took him to the boys' school and then to the girls' school. Robins thought this was wonderful work and was so impressed with Father Barnum that he told him he should be in the United States where he could accomplish more. The priest quietly replied that he must follow God's will. "Ours is to do our duty; results are in higher hands." Robins said to himself, "This priest has something I haven't. I couldn't be satisfied to spend my life among a lot of half-breeds."

After they left the Catholic mission, his comrade developed snow blindness and wanted to die. For the first time Robins prayed, and eventually they found their way to an Indian village which provided them with warmth, food, and shelter.

They went on and reached the gold regions, and there Robins struck it rich. After working a while, he decided to go down to Juneau to get some machinery. When he reached there, he found that the next boat back did not leave for four days. He decided to do something worthwhile and borrowed the only New Testament he could find from a girl living in the community. He read through all four Gospels. The next day he went back and read all of Matthew, Mark, and Luke, and then in the seventh chapter of John he found these words: "If any man willeth to do God's will, he shall *know* of the doctrine."

Robins said to himself, "Hell, I don't know if there is any God. But if there *is* a God, and He *has* a will for me, and I can do it, I'd be a damn fool not to do it." He decided to start right away, and that night he prayed: "I want to do Your will, if You are God, and I want to test it out myself."

The next morning he found a man who was going up to where his partner was, and he paid him to take up the machinery. He then went over to Douglas Island and offered to work for the pastor for nothing. The minister asked him if he were a Christian. When Robins said he didn't know, the minister said he couldn't take anybody who wasn't a Christian to work in the church. Robins handed over a bag with $800 in it and said, "If while I am with you, I cost you anything or do any harm to any of your work, pay yourself out of that." The result was that he went to live with the minister.

Finding that none of the miners came to church, he persuaded them to come to the service. But the sermon was over their heads so the pastor finally asked Robins to address them. He made such effective sermons that the pastor asked him to go as a missionary to the Nome area. Robins accepted the offer and opened a church at St. Michael's Island, and then at Nome. Here he built a hospital as well. This was used as a school in the morning and afternoon and as a library from 4 *p.m.* until 9 *p.m.* By this time he was already ordained as a minister.

Soon Robins found that there was graft and corruption in the municipal government, and he called together a mass meeting which succeeded in securing the resignations of the grafters and installing an honest regime.

Finally, Robins went back to his claim, and in his first washing took out $7,000 worth of gold. Eventually, he had over a quarter of a million dollars in gold and returned to the States.

He stopped to see his cousins with whom he had lived in Florida. Their daughter had married Frank Hogan, a millionaire, who was planning to go to Pasadena, California. Raymond Robins commented: "Their whole attitude of life was utterly alien to mine. And they would have said that they had religion and I didn't. What they had was to go to church and then do as they damned pleased."

In 1900, Robins went to Chicago and started work in a particularly poor section called "The Bloody 17th Ward."

He wrote: "I learned so much about the indifference of the rich and privileged to the poor and miserable in a great city, perhaps the richest in the world and in the richest land in the world. I found a whole section where 75,000 people could be exploited and robbed and in bad health. And the fact that the community was going to hell didn't bother them at all." He set out to reform the situation and finally with the cooperation of others, elected Mayor Dever to do the job.

He also aided in the establishment of three important institutions: The Settlement Organization, a municipal lodging house; and the City Homes Association.

He tried particularly to help the downtrodden and the poverty stricken. He naturally became increasingly aware of the flaws in American society. He fought the "Gray Wolf Gang." He saw the large-scale graft, the crime, and the prostitution which was being perpetrated under "Hinky Dink" Mike Kenna, an alderman who controlled the Loop district.

When he left Alaska, he had determined that he would give one third of his time and his money to the economic struggle, another third to the social control of the government, and the rest "to the religious sanction in the human heart."

He had also determined that he would never marry, since his way of life would be too difficult for a woman. However, he was invited to speak at Henry Ward Beecher's church in New York City, and at every luncheon he attended on this trip, there was a very attractive girl present,—Margaret Dreier.

When he got back to Chicago, he made up his mind to marry her and he took $5,000 of his savings and returned to New York. There he saw Margaret, told her the entire story of his life, and proposed marriage. Margaret Dreier accepted immediately, and they were married in June, 1905, returning to Chicago to live in a tenement house in the slums. Margaret Dreier was a great help to Raymond Robins. She fitted admirably into his vision and outlook and gave him inspiration and help all along the way.[1]

Robins was always working for the interests of the people. In 1907, he campaigned for Mark Fagan of Jersey City against the vested interests. In 1910, he was appointed to the Arbitration Commission that settled the strike of the Philadelphia Rapid Transit Company. He frequently helped in organizing and conducting strikes to promote justice for the workers. Both Robins and his wife were bound and determined to get a decent living wage for workingmen and women, shorter hours, safe and sanitary working conditions, and always the right to organize and bargain collectively. Of course, they were opposed to child labor. Robins tried to help in the Williamson County coal strike where a large number of miners had been killed but was unable to get any convictions for murder in spite of the clear evidence.

As far back as 1908 he spoke with prophetic insight to the Chicago Federation of Labor in favor of union labor and the eight-hour day. He said, "The most careful inquiry that was ever made into the effects of the hours of labor upon the production of wealth justifies the conclusion that for a period of five years without change in the workers, an eight-hour day will produce more net material wealth than a ten-hour day." Robins believed also that shorter hours aided citizenship. In conclusion he said, "I am one

[1] The story of her life and devoted service in many fields is told in *Margaret Dreier Robins* by Mary E. Dreier. She was one of the pioneers in legislation to protect women in industry.

of those who, knowing the power of the worst in our human life, believe absolutely in the triumph of the best. I believe that the love of freedom, justice, and righteousness of the whole people is safe against the machinations of the group of plunderers now and forever . . . we are now engaged in the third great struggle in the life of this nation, the struggle for industrial freedom."

One of the great achievements of Robins was his evangelistic work. He was a persuasive, challenging, provocative, and inspiring natural orator, with a clear Christian purpose. On the campuses of our great colleges, he would hold an audience enthralled for an hour and a half. Then most of the students would remain for the forum period. He would sometimes begin his engagements in Texas, then continue up through Arizona, California, Oregon, and Washington. He would tell of his personal adventures in Alaska and of the social-economic-political struggles in the 17th Ward in Chicago.

Between engagements, on the trains, Raymond would read the Bible, pray, and spend time in thought.

Fred B. Smith was the leader of the "Men and Religion Movement." He had never met Robins but thought of him as a "dangerous radical." When an organizing conference was held at Silver Bay in 1911, Robins was present, but Smith was determined not to let him have a place on the program. However, the demands of the six hundred delegates to hear Robins were so great that he was allowed to conduct the twenty-minute "devotional period" for one day. Smith said; "He made the most profound impression of any man in the entire eight days' sessions." This resulted in his appointment to one of the teams. Conventions were held in seventy-seven major cities of the country, culminating in a great convention in Carnegie Hall in April,

1912. The campaign was so successful that in 1913 a world tour was organized which lasted from January to July. From then up to July 1932, there were campaigns in behalf of law enforcement and world peace. Fred B. Smith said of Robins, "I have been with him in literally thousands of conventions and conferences." He went on to say that, among all the leaders with whom he had worked, "I have not found one who reads his Bible so persistently and who says his prayers to God so regularly as did this great crusader."

Robins went all out for Theodore Roosevelt's campaign for the presidency in 1912 and did everything possible to assure his election.

In July of 1917, through the influence of ex-President Theodore Roosevelt, Raymond Robins was sent as a member of the Red Cross Commission to Russia by President Wilson, with the rank of major. There, the present writer saw him frequently. He acted as unofficial representative of the American Ambassador to Russia in conversations and negotiations with the Soviet Government. During this period, he saw Lenin on the average of three times a week.

I know personally that Raymond Robins was opposed to communism, because we discussed the matter. William Hard, the nationally known writer, wrote: "Robins is the most anti-Bolshevik person I have ever known in way of thought; and I have known him for seventeen years."

In various ways Robins tried to help the United States of America. Trotsky proposed that a United States railway commission come into Russia and offered to appoint a member of this commission as assistant superintendent of Russian Ways and Communications in order to help evacuate war supplies from the front so that the Germans would not capture them. Robins went to the American diplomats with this proposal, but they believed that communism was going to be overthrown by Russian generals and would do nothing.

Robins got Lenin to agree that the Russians might continue the war against Germany if they could get any assurance that the United States would help them. He had tried to get the United States to recognize the new Bolshevik government but had failed. When the Bolsheviks were forced by their tragic situation to consider making peace with Germany, Robins persuaded them to send a message to the President in Washington, offering to continue the war if economic help were forthcoming and if Japan were not allowed to attack Siberia. Even U.S. Ambassador Francis had sent a cable to Washington in which he said, "I cannot too strongly urge the folly of intervention by the Japanese just now. It is possible that the Congress of Soviets may ratify the peace, but if I receive assurance from you that the Japanese peril is baseless, I am of the opinion that the Congress will reject this humiliating peace."

While President Wilson sent a cable to the Congress of Soviets on March 14th expressing sympathy "for the Russian people," he said the Government of the United States would not give them direct aid.

The awful consequence of this was that the Brest-Litovsk peace was made by the Soviets with Germany, and thus many divisions of German troops were transferred to the Western front, and the World War dragged on for another year. It also resulted in Ambassador Francis' wiring the State Department on May 2, 1918, urging Allied intervention in Russia. Ambassador Francis believed that if the Allies attacked, the people would rise and the communists would be overthrown. He was entirely mistaken.

On May 7th, Robins received a cable asking him to return to the United States. When he came, he carried a proposal from the Bolshevik government offering a monopoly on the platinum mines in Russia until the debt owed the United States was paid. Our government refused this offer, and as a result never did receive any compensation. Of course, our military intervention was also a colossal failure.

General William V. Judson, military attache of the American Embassy, expressed what happened: "All American aid to the Russian people is at a standstill, while the German emissaries are everywhere, working day and night in the interests of the enemy."

Lockhart, representing the British Government, was in full agreement with Robins. Lockhart was instructed by his government "to go the limit in cooperation" with the Soviets, but the United States was opposed to this.

It was not until 1933, when Franklin Delano Roosevelt was president, that Col. Robins again went to Russia where he was received by Stalin and other officials. On his return, he urged the recognition of the U.S.S.R. for humanitarian and strategic reasons and this step was finally taken.

On this trip to Russia in 1933, Robins was impressed by the tremendous progress that had been made. Russian workers were throwing themselves into the industrialization of their backward country. He believed that the vast majority of the peasantry were favorable to collectivization. In many places where there had been nothing, factories or dams had been built. He believed that Soviet children were being better cared for than, perhaps, any others in the world. He found the condition of the Russian people vastly improved.

In his interview with Stalin, Robins said: "The situation forces us above all to follow our own interests . . . We are interested in the development of American exports. The only big market with great possibilities . . . is the Russian market."

Time has proved Robins' predictions about Russia correct. The U.S.S.R. today has emerged as perhaps the second strongest nation in the world.

Raymond Robins was an ardent advocate of the outlawing of war. He campaigned for it all over the country. President Harding had said in an address in 1920, "If I catch the conscience of America, we'll lead the world to outlaw war." In 1921, together with Levinson of Chicago, Robins helped to form the American Committee for the Outlawry of War. The Federal Council of Churches adopted a resolution to outlaw war and worked actively for its realization. In 1922, all through the summer and fall, Robins was "spreading this gospel like a flame . . . devouring prairies and cities alike." On August 9, 1922 he wrote to Levinson that four thousand people from all parts of the United States had heard him speak on the outlawry of war.

In July, 1924, through the influence of William Jennings Byran, Robins was able to get the outlawry program written into the Democratic platform. At the annual convention of the American Academy of Political and Social Science in 1925, Robins spoke on "The Outlawry of War — the Next Step in Civilization." In 1926, he continued to lecture all over the country on this theme. Eventually an outlawry pact was signed by the United States, France, Germany, Italy, Japan, Poland, Belgium,

Czechoslovakia, Ireland, and Great Britain. On January 15, 1929, it was ratified by the Senate in a vote of 85 to 1. Nevertheless, there was some truth to Rabbi Stephen Wise's characterization of it as "a wishbone rather than a backbone for peace." On July 24, 1929, President Hoover solemnly declared the pact in effect. Of course, Russia had not signed because she was not then recognized by the United States and had not been brought into the discussion. The outbreak of World War II proved that mere outlawry is not enough to prevent conflict.

No wonder Robins received signal honors during his lifetime. He was awarded honorary degrees from George Washington University, Hillsdale College, and the University of Florida. He had a will of iron which he used no matter what the difficulties and obstacles. During his life he was: Member of the Chicago Board of Education, Chairman of the State Central Committee of the Progressive Party, Superintendent of the Chicago Municipal Lodging House, Head Worker of Northwestern University Settlement, Trustee and Charter Member of The Theodore Roosevelt Memorial Association, Vice-Chairman of the National Committee for the Outlawry of War, Member of the Men and Religion Forward Movement, and Moderator of the National Council of Congregational Churches.

Probably the most important single accomplishment of his life was the inspiration he gave when speaking to young men in colleges in every part of the nation. I can well remember the impression he made on the students when I was teaching at Dartmouth College. Some of them said they would never forget his message. A Florida lawyer has said, "He liberalized my entire outlook in life." Undoubtedly, the guiding purpose of his life was to help the "underdog," the poverty-stricken and the exploited.

In doing this he often ran into great opposition. In the South he sometimes faced bitter hostility from those who were opposed to his stand on equality and justice for the Negro. At his beautiful home on the hill at Chinsegut (Brooksville, Florida) he held religious services every Sunday morning and always had both Negroes and whites of the household in attendance. He had a colored chauffeur, and once the local Ku Klux Klan appeared, and, not finding him, seized his brother whom they beat up, and told him that the chauffeur was never to come back. Once the Ku Klux Klan burned his barn, including his horse and wagon, because he employed Fielder who was the old colored man who had done so much to help him in his youth.

In September of 1935 as Raymond Robins was pruning a tree, one of the branches broke. He fell and broke his back which resulted in paralysis from the waist down. He was crippled for the remainder of his life. This did not prevent great helpfulness to others, especially those who were working for social justice, until his death on September 26, 1954.

No brief chapter can do justice to Raymond Robins and his life, but perhaps it can challenge us to stop, to ponder, and to pray for our own shortcomings.

Raymond Robins was a crusader, a prophet, and a great religious leader. He was a man of absolute *sincerity*. He hated sham and could not endure hypocrisy. Fred B. Smith stated: "Of all the men with whom I have worked in many years of public life, I do not remember one that I could mark higher than I could this noble man for his unbiased and untarnished sincerity."

No one could possibly deny that he had *courage*. Fred B. Smith continued: "More than once in his life where great issues were at stake, and where hoodlums and gang-dom were stuffing ballot boxes, packing juries, debauching courts,—he would walk in, with his rather frail-looking body but with bare fists,—and break up the mob. More than once in such experiences he was beaten up, slugged, and carried to hospitals, where he might have his broken bones and wounds healed."

He had *moral courage,* and if he thought something was right, nothing could deter him from championing it.

He had prophetic insight. He saw that the Soviet Union must be recognized and never gave up the fight until this was done under President Roosevelt.

As we have seen, he had a profound *religious life.* In the entire Men and Religion Forward Movement no one of the leaders did such effective religious work as Raymond Robins. Fred B. Smith recalled that in their tour around the world: "Everyone in the party has spoken to me repeatedly of their memory of the great spiritual impression made by Raymond Robins."

Every reader should be challenged by his life and character. Raymond Robins is dead, but his courage, his sincerity, his devotion to social justice, his sacrificial life for others should continue to move each one of us to do everything we can for God and the common good.

VII

DR. HARRY EMERSON FOSDICK

ONE OF THE GREAT teachers at Union Theological Seminary has been Dr. Harry Emerson Fosdick. In his homiletical course he would not only lecture but he would have us deliver sermons and then criticize them constructively and challengingly. His sermons and talks gripped the hearts and minds of us all.

Dr. Fosdick was born on May 24, 1878, in Buffalo. At that time the United States was largely a nation of farmers with nearly forty of the fifty million population living in the open spaces. It was only two years before that an inventor had showed the first crude model of a telephone which was laughed at as an impossible fake.

At that time many regarded public schools as "creeping socialism" and Fosdick's grandfather carried on a fight against that kind of spurious thinking. His father was a teacher in the Buffalo schools. When Harry was five, the family had twins, Edith and Raymond. When he was seven, his mother had a severe case of nervous prostration. Harry joined the Baptist Church in spite of the fact that the family thought he was too young. He decided then to be a missionary. In 1895, he graduated from high school. At that time the Turks had been massacring the Armenians, and in his graduation oration, he made an appeal for those decimated people. On Sundays he went to a Bible class in the Presbyterian Church.

Harry had his weaknesses as other boys do. Once he stole a chicken and roasted it with the other boys. The next day they picked berries for the owner and refused to take any pay so they salved their consciences.

Harry knew about the Haymarket riot in Chicago in 1886, the Homestead battle between the steel workers and Pinkerton's men in Pittsburgh in 1892, and the poverty of the people in the great depression of 1893. In general his parents were on the side of the underdog. His father once, looking at his monthly pay check, commented that although it wasn't large he could count on it while millions had nothing. Fosdick later wrote that the potential dangers of America are "obvious money-madness, crude and loutish standards of success, and all the evils of a crass materialism." He said, "I thank God that I was reared in a family where spiritual values were cherished and conserved."

Fosdick went to Colgate College. At the end of his freshman year his father suffered a nervous breakdown and to conserve the family finances, the son stayed at home and took at job at four dollars a week in a bookstore. While at home he taught a Sunday school class and came to the conclusion that he could not regard all the stories in the Bible, like those about Samson for instance, as objective and valid.

During this year at home he read the two-volume work of Andrew D. White, *History of the Warfare of Science with Theology in Christendom,* and this reinforced his conclusion that some of the Biblical stories were not necessarily historical.

When Harry returned to college the next year, he refused to go either to church or Sunday school. A prayer circle in the Y.M.C.A. used to pray for his return to the faith, but this did not change him. At the beginning of his junior year he told his mother, "I'll behave as though there is a God, but mentally I'm going to clear God out of the Universe and start all over again." Gradually he came to the conviction that there must be some way of being both intelligent and Christian. Before he returned to college for his senior year, his father said to him, "Harry, you know that you will never be satisfied outside the Christian ministry." This helped him come to a decision.

After graduation he was awarded a scholarship to a theological seminary and also won a prize of $250 in a state vivisection contest. This enabled him to enter the Divinity School at Colgate in 1900 without being a burden on the family. Here he was profoundly affected by Prof. William Newton Clarke who stressed personal rather than theological religion. After one year he went to Union Theological Seminary and while studying helped run the mission for the "down-and-outers" on the Bowery. He sometimes held as many as nine meetings in Bowery lodginghouses in a single Sunday. In November, he had a nervous breakdown and was sent to Europe for six weeks by his future father-in-law. Because of this, prayer became a deeper experience. In his senior year in the Seminary he became a student assistant at the Madison Avenue Baptist Church. Here he was ordained on November 18, 1903. He graduated *summa cum laude*.

He then accepted the pastorate of the First Baptist Church of Montclair, New Jersey. During the August vacation he was married to Florence Whitney. It wasn't long before he was invited to preach in the college chapels at Harvard, Princeton, Yale, and elsewhere. He found it a thrilling adventure, and one cannot estimate the far-reaching effects of his challenge to students.

Throughout his life he wrote books which had wide

circulation. *The Manhood of the Master* was translated into many languages. *The Meaning of Prayer,* was translated into seventeen languages. He soon decided that a sermon should not be a lecture but a constructive concern for the real problems of the people in his audience. In effect he tried to make his sermons a form of personal counseling to meet the problems of those who were at his services.

I remember in his classroom at Union, his telling about the minister who had begun his sermon in a school chapel, when a professor arose from the audience, mounted the pulpit, and offered a criticism of what had been said. The audience was electrified. The minister answered the criticism of the professor but the latter remained in the pulpit and the resulting dialogue between the two became a sermon. Of course, all this had been prearranged but it made a tremendous impression on the students. Fosdick said you could not stage such a program easily but you could try to face people's real problems, meet their difficulties, and answer their questions.

I was interested in his opinion of great leaders. He said, "Gandhi has been one of my heroes, he will remain an unforgettable character in man's spiritual history; I wish more than I can say, that I could have the privilege of meeting him." He was strongly influenced by Walter Rauschenbusch, exponent of the "social gospel." Rauschenbusch was pastor of a little church in "Hell's Kitchen" in New York City. As he said, his social outlook came "through personal contact with poverty, and when I saw how men toiled all their life long, hard, hard toilsome lives, and at the end had almost nothing to show for it; how strong men begged for work and could not get it in hard times; how little children died." After seeing the famous textile strike in Lawrence, Massachusetts, in 1912, Fosdick became convinced that trade unions were necessary.

When the First World War broke out, he was for it and wrote *The Challenge of the Present Crisis,* defending the war. Fosdick later said it was "the only book I ever wrote that I wish had not been written." By World War II Dr. Fosdick had become a pacifist and made the following pledge:

> I can never use my Christian Ministry for the support and sanction of war . . . When I picture Christ in this warring world, I can see Him in one place only, not arrayed in the panoply of battle on either side, but on His judgment seat, sitting in condemnation on all of us, —aggressor, defender, neutral,—who by our joint guilt have involved ourselves in a way of life that denies everything He stood for. The function of the church is to keep Him there above the strife, representing a manner of living, the utter antithesis of war, to which mankind must return if we are to have any hope.

Gradually, personal and social ethics became the major concern of Dr. Fosdick.

In the summer of 1921, the Fosdicks went to Japan and China. He came to the conclusion that it was largely the West that was responsible for the loss of China. He said: "The angry spirit of revolt, especially against Western foreigners, was flaming ever higher, and it was justified. If now the so-called "free nations" have lost China, the basic reason goes far back to the arrogant humiliations,—the opium wars, the unequal treaties, the extraterritorial rights, the insolent assumption of racial superiority, the signs like *No Chinese, no dogs allowed,* and all the rest to which the Western foreigners had long subjected the Chinese. No wonder that even when I was there in 1921 the Bolshevik revolution in Russia was making a strong appeal to China."[1]

When preaching at the First Presbyterian Church in New York, Dr. Fosdick came under attack from the Fundamentalists. Although he had many supporters, the General Assembly of the First Presbyterian Church finally adopted a moderate resolution asking him to become a Presbyterian. Dr. Fosdick decided not to do this and resigned from the Church. Meanwhile the New York *Times* came to his defense in an editorial which said among other things: "It is plain that the whole loss will not fall upon Dr. Fosdick, but upon the Presbyterian Church. It will have convicted itself in the eyes of the lay public not only of a certain denominational narrowness, but of the folly of giving up the services of a preacher whose good report has filled the entire city, become known throughout the entire country, and reached the knowledge of the churches of England."

Dr. Fosdick then accepted an appointment as Minister of the Park Avenue Baptist Church which later became the new Riverside Church with the help of John D. Rockefeller, Jr. The Church was dedicated in 1931 and became nonsectarian, welcoming members from any denominational background. It also accepted everyone regardless of race, color, or nationality. Actually Chinese, Japanese, Jews, Negroes, Slavs, and South Americans of various nationalities are in its membership. The Church has ten kitchens, and from ten to fifteen thousand people come weekly to its activities. Counseling has been a central work of the Church and Dr. Fosdick tries to help every member with his or her problems. He says that this has been all-

[1] Harry Emerson Fosdick, *The Living of These Days.* (New York: Harper & Brothers) , p. 137.

important in his ministry, and as we have noted even in his sermons, he has tried to do personal counseling on a group scale.

He has any number of illustrations of individual problems. One is of a young man who had tried to commit suicide. Dr. Fosdick learned that in his boyhood days, a brutal father used to beat him mercilessly until his back was covered with welts. The boy developed feelings of "shame, self-scorn and humiliation." Dr. Fosdick was able to show him that he had "admirable qualities" and later on the young man became a success and even was praised in a trade journal for his effective work.

Dr. Fosdick recognizes that our best good is often corroded by egocentricity and pride. He points out that "Christianity has grown soft, sentimental, saccharine. It has taken on pink flesh and lost strong bone," but he believes: "We do experience sin, guilty remorse, and forgiveness; and moral victory, snatched from the jaws of defeat by the influx of a Power greater than our own, is as real an event as sunrise."

While Dr. Fosdick realizes that Christianity has often given "divine sanction to such monstrous evils as slavery, racial discrimination, war and religious persecution as being 'the will of God,' " nevertheless, he says, "Mankind desperately needs what Christianity at its best has to offer."

Today, science has given man tremendous power, but "power is never a good, except he be good that has it." He quotes Charles Lindbergh: "I have seen the science I worshipped and the aircraft that I loved destroying the civilization I expected them to serve, while the lifesaving miracles of medicine are being perverted toward the murderous ends of biological warfare." Dr. Fosdick says, "There is only one thing worse than a devil and that is an educated devil." He quotes Compton, the Nobel Prize winner: "Science has created a world in which Christianity is an imperative."

Fosdick believes that ultimately civilization's success or failure "is to be found in what happens to the underdog." This has always haunted his preaching. In our struggle against communism we must remember that this is precisely what the communists themselves believe. They would subscribe wholeheartedly to his statement, "The downtrodden reveal the unjust wrongs and cruelties of any social order, and what happens to them is, in the long run, any social order's test." In our struggle against communism we have to prove that we are doing this better than they.

Fosdick declares that as far back as 1890 one percent of the people in the United States owned more than the remaining ninety-nine percent. He declares "that is an insane situation" and concludes: "In the long fight, therefore, to make government the servant of all the people, I have been on the liberal side." He challenges our thinking with these words:

> It is not the underprivileged, the whipped and beaten, who have brought on the world its greatest evils. No! Privilege is power, and privilege consolidated in a social class is prodigious power, and the misuse of *that* especially to sustain an unjust *status quo* grown obsolete has been, I suspect, responsible for the worst wrongs that have cursed mankind.

Dr. Fosdick has always been fearless in championing what he believed to be right. For instance, when Professor MacIntosh of Yale Divinity School was denied his United States citizenship by the U.S. Supreme Court in a four to five decision, because he would not promise to support any war, just or unjust, Fosdick vigorously protested the decision and lost from his church one "of our leading lawyers, who stalked out and never came back."

Dr. Fosdick would go out of his way to help anyone. When the present writer, along with the Secretary of Labor in the Roosevelt cabinet and John L. Lewis of the United Mine Workers, was attacked by a prominent periodical, he brought suit for libel. Dr. Fosdick generously took time to testify in his behalf, and it was the first time he had ever testified in a courtroom. The outcome was that this writer received vindication and damages.

Always concerned about injustice, Fosdick took action against the miscarriages of justice in the Sacco-Vanzetti Case in Massachusetts, the Mooney Case in California, and the Scottsboro Case in Alabama. He tells how Ruby Bates, one of the girls who testified at the first trial of the Scottsboro Case, crept into his study and confessed that she had lied at the trial, and it was a white boy "she had lain with," and that the Negro had not touched her. Dr. Fosdick persuaded her to go back and confess her perjury at the second trial. This she did but it had no effect on the Alabama jury, and nineteen years went by before, as Dr. Fosdick says, "the last of those falsely accused boys was released from prison."

In fact, the struggle against racial discrimination and against mistreatment of the Negro has been a lifelong concern of Dr. Fosdick. He believed in the remark of John Wesley that American slavery was "the vilest that ever saw the sun." It is a testimonial to Dr. Fosdick's life and character that at Riverside Church, there is a statue of Booker T. Washington, carved in stone and placed among the sculptures in the chancel.

On the question of war, Dr. Fosdick completely reversed

the opinion which he held at the beginning of his ministry. He quotes outstanding leaders such as John Ruskin who said: "War is the foundation of all the arts . . . of all the high virtues and faculties of men" but he also quotes General Eisenhower who declared: "I hate war as only a soldier who has lived in it can, only as one who has seen its brutality, its futility, its stupidity." He recognizes that while some pacifists are "wrongheaded," ministers who champion war may be "grossly betraying the Christian faith, prostituting their ministry to the service of a false god until the distinctive elements of the Christian ethic are obliterated." Dr. Fosdick, therefore, prefers to be enrolled with the pacifists. In World War II he was prepared, if asked, to resign from his church, to join the Quakers and spend the rest of his life in their fellowship. He did join the Wider Quaker Fellowship.

In regard to communism Dr. Fosdick points out that at least it proclaims "a gospel of change. This world is all wrong, it says, and we are out to transform it. In consequence, along with some starry-eyed idealists, millions of impoverished, discontented, exploited people around the world welcome communist propaganda, if only because it promises them one thing they want most—a change. I certainly am anti-communist—anti its totalitarianism, its atheism, its Marxism—but I am also sure that the only way to beat the communists is to match and surpass them in proclaiming a new day for the world's common people."

Dr. Fosdick rightly says that our democratic ancestors were the progressives. "They stirred the world with a gospel of revolutionary change; they were the apostles of a new day. We betray our forefathers if we let that desire for security and static changelessness in so stormy an era, crush out that spirit."

In order to truly understand the meaning of Dr. Harry Emerson Fosdick's life and service, you must hear him speak and you must read his books. As a student I was profoundly impressed by his sincerity, by his dedication, and by his willingness to give everything within him for what he believed would channel love of God into any personal or collective need anywhere in the world. We who are reading these words must transform our own lives and give everything we have to serve the common good. Let us take from the life of Harry Emerson Fosdick the fire of his sincerity and let us devote as he did all our energy, all our moments for the benefit of the people.

VIII

SIDNEY HILLMAN

SIDNEY HILLMAN WAS one of the labor leaders that I saw quite frequently when I was teaching at the Yale University Divinity School. As a matter of fact, I was interviewing him when my daughter aged five and one half, was shot by the seven-year-old son of a Y.M.C.A. secretary. The boy took down a loaded rifle from the wall in his home, pulled the trigger, and the bullet went right through her body. She was on the danger list for several days.

The sincerity and ability of Sidney Hillman always impressed me. Every visit with him brought inspiration. His challenging work for labor added fuel to my efforts to start the National Religion and Labor Foundation. I began paying for this work out of my own pocket and it has been going forward ever since with remarkable results and now has a headquarters in Washington D. C.

It has always seemed to me that every American boy should read and know something about the life and work of Sidney Hillman, because it would challenge him to do constructive and positive work for the welfare of the people of his own time.

Sidney Hillman was born March 23, 1887 in Zagare, a village in Lithuania, the second of seven children. His father was an orthodox Jew who bought grain and milled it into flour which he then sold. His business was not very prosperous so later his wife opened a small grocery store in the front room of their house. From the age of five Sidney had to attend a Bible class every day. Here he had to read and memorize the scriptures.

When he was fourteen, the family sent him to Yeshiva (Jewish Seminary) at Kovno to become a rabbi. After a year there he wanted to study Russian and its literature. Hillman received only three dollars a month for food, so he couldn't pay anything for lessons, but another boy offered to teach him free. So Hillman walked three miles each day for the Russian studies. He soon found that the home where he was going was a center for illegal trade-union and revolutionary activity.

When the Chief Rabbi of the Yeshiva learned that Hillman was taking Russian lessons, he called him in and told him he must either stop the lessons or leave the school. Sidney continued his lessons and was again called before the Rabbi and this time his father was also there to reinforce the plea. It was all to no avail, and Sidney left the Yeshiva. He earned his way by cleaning the laboratory and running errands for the chemist at whose home he was studying.

The Jewish labor movement had been crushed by the Tsar's police in 1902, but it was rising again and Hillman volunteered to work under the outlawed trade-union leaders. On May 1, 1904, he led a group of one hundred workingmen in a demonstration down the main street of the town. He was immediately seized by the police and held for months without trial. As was usual under the Tsar's tyranny, he was beaten until he lost consciousness, then cold water was poured over him until he revived, and then the beating was resumed. He was released after five months and resumed his revolutionary work. In the uprisings of 1905, he was again arrested, but the Tsar's proclamation of amnesty set him free after four months. His parents begged him to leave the country, but he wanted to take part in freeing Russia.

By the summer of 1906, however, it was apparent that the Revolution was failing. The Tsar had dissolved the Duma (parliament), and Hillman agreed to go. He secured a false passport and managed to get over the border and went to Manchester, England, where his uncle lived. He stayed there for nine months and then decided to go to the United States. In August, 1907, he arrived in New York. The Tsar's tyranny had forged the makings of a great labor union leader by the time he was nineteen.

In Chicago, Sidney secured a job in Sears Roebuck, packing clothing in parcels, at a salary of eight dollars a week for sixty hours of work. One day one of the men working at the table with him, who had a wife and two children, was laid off. This shocked Hillman; he even thought of going to the foreman and offering to leave in place of the other man but was told by the workers that this would do no good at all. He came to the conclusion: "There is something terribly wrong with this system." He decided then and there to devote himself to the labor movement in America.

There were 7,000 girls in Sears Roebuck, working ten hours a day plus three nights a week for a total of 70 hours a week. When a slump came in 1909, he was discharged and went to work for Hart, Shaffner and Marx. He had to work six weeks without pay while he was learning his job, and after that he received only six dollars weekly.

In Russia, Hillman had experienced the Tsar's tyranny, and now he saw that millions of workers in the United States also lived in insecurity and fear. He began to attend organizing meetings of the clothing workers in Chicago.

Hillman believed that we had "industrial slavery" in the United States. He would quote Abraham Lincoln that a nation could not remain "half slave and half free," and he felt that in our country, we could not be "free politically and slaves industrially."

In 1910 the garment manufacturers tried to cut the piece rate for seaming pants from four to three and three-quarter cents per piece. Some of the workers quit. Hillman joined the walkout and manned the picket line. Four hundred workers were placed under arrest, and one of the pickets was shot and killed. Finally, they won the right to arbitrate the strike. In 1911 Hillman became the business agent of the newly formed Chicago local of the United Garment Workers of America.

At this time he received only fifteen dollars a week as a union official. In 1914 he was offered a position in New York with the International Ladies Garment Workers Union. This meant that he would represent 50,000 women's garment workers before the Board of Conciliation. He decided to accept. He was already engaged to Bessie Abramowitz who had been a tireless worker for the union and business agent for one of the locals.

At the national convention of the United Garment Workers in Nashville in 1914, there was a sudden ruling that unions which had not paid their dues in full to the national union would be denied representation. This meant that delegates representing almost two thirds of the membership were denied voting rights. The result was that those who were excluded decided to form their own industrial union. They offered Sidney Hillman the presidency, and he accepted.

The first report written by Hillman and Joseph Schlossberg in 1914 had this to say: "Our path, as you know, was not strewn with roses when we returned from our convention at Nashville to New York to take hold of the business of our union. We had to enter upon our duties without a cent in the treasury, without even an office or stationery."

During the first year of Hillman's work there were between 35,000 and 38,000 members in his union. A convention of the seceding workers was called in New York on December 26, 1914, and the Amalgamated Clothing Workers of America was formed. It discarded the crafts structure and adopted industrial organization. In its first two years the Amalgamated participated in a series of losing strikes even while its membership was increasing. By 1916 they had secured a three-year agreement with Hart, Schaffner and Marx. Eventually the other 20,000 workers in the garment trade in Chicago also joined the Amalgamated.

Sidney Hillman and Bessie Abramowitz were married on May 3, 1916 in Chicago. Bessie resigned her position as business agent of Local No. 152 and joined him in New York. She realized that Sidney would devote all his time to the union but she believed in the work so firmly that she did not care. In fact in 1924 when she bought an old grand piano and installed it in the house, Sidney never noticed it for six months.

When the First World War broke, Hillman advocated full support for it but demanded that all government contracts refuse "to permit conditions which make for the breaking down of the standard of labor established in our industry through many sacrifices and bitter struggles. . . ."

With the coming of peace, Hillman decided to plan a grand offensive "to start an agitation throughout the country for the establishment of the 44-hour week." A million dollars was to be raised to finance possible general strikes in cities. This was to be secured by assessments on members' wages. Since the American Federation of Labor was only working for the 8-hour day, this meant that the Amalgamated was the first union in the United States to call for the 44-hour week. On January 7, 1919 Hillman concluded a new agreement with Hart, Schaffner and Marx, granting an average increase of 8¾ cents and the 44-hour week. Naturally the union grew by leaps and bounds. By the end of 1919 it had roughly a half-million dollars in its treasury. When the steel strike began in 1919, Sidney Hillman immediately donated $100,000 for the relief of the steel strikers. It was the largest gift of the sort ever made by a union.

In the 1920 convention of the Amalgamated, the delegates voted overwhelmingly for unemployment insurance and for the union to undertake cooperative enterprises such as cooperative banks.

When they tried to unionize Michaels, Stern & Co. in Rochester, the company made a deal with a rival union, The United Garment Workers. Sidney Hillman called a strike, and the company secured an injunction which forbade all strike action. Hillman then secured the cooperation of Prof. Felix Frankfurter, who was teaching at Harvard Law School, as their attorney. Frankfurter offered to take the case without compensation if the union would plead its case as a defense of all unions in America. Hillman readily agreed. The union spent $100,000 on the trial but lost the decision.

Actually this case probably was instrumental in the enactment of the Norris-LaGuardia Anti-Injunction Act which came a decade later.

When the employers began an "open-shop" drive against the organized workers, Hillman fought it with everything in his power. He stated: "Open shop means arbitrary dictation. Open shop means the un-American way; open shop means employing the methods of the Kaiser, the Tsar, and every other autocrat. Open shop means starvation, death. Open shop means the slums; it means crime; it means asylums; it means everything that is rotten, everything that is inhuman. . . . It means a citizenship that has no time to think, the 7-day week, the 12-hour day in the steel mills. It means Lawrence. It means the East Side."

The result was that in spite of the depression the employers could not get the workers that they needed. When the manufacturers tried to get a resolution in the Senate to investigate the Amalgamated Clothing Workers, Senator William E. Borah immediately introduced a resolution calling for an investigation of "the profits in the manufacture and sale of clothing during the past seven years . . . with special reference to the contracting system and sweatshops." This caused the clothing manufacturers to cancel their demand for a legislative investigation.

The result of the strike was a final settlement with the 44-hour week, the union shop, and the adjustment of grievances. Sidney Hillman had won the battle against the employers.

On April 14, 1923, Sidney Hillman opened the first labor bank in New York City which became known as the Amalgamated Bank of New York. Another had been opened in Chicago in 1922. Both were very successful.

In 1921 Hillman went to Europe to see his parents in Lithuania for the first time since he had left years before. He then helped send relief to the people who were starving there. He also saw Lenin and was deeply impressed with his sincerity and leadership. He was convinced that Lenin's group was the only one that could hold the country together and that the overthrow of communism would only "produce chaos."

Hillman was always generous in spirit and wanted to help meet the needs of people so he formed a Russian-American Industrial Corporation which was to produce clothing in Russia. He went back to Russia in 1922 and negotiated an agreement with the Soviet Government that the principal and interest were to be guaranteed by the Russians. In the end, $300,000 was put into the project.

Sidney Hillman was very much opposed to intervention in Russia by the United States and other powers. At the Amalgamated Convention in 1922 he spoke out against this in the following words:

"You do not commit murder only when you go out in the street and kill someone; you commit murder when you make it impossible for other people to live. . .

"The great danger is that the peoples are indifferent . . . and it will all result in part of the world trying to choke the other. When that happens there will be very little left in the world worth living for. It is up to the people in this country, as well as in every other country, to rise and say that . . . the lives of millions of men, women and children are the concern of all the people.

"When a great conflagration strikes a community it disregards all petty divisions of groups and classes. . . . Disease and fire have their own laws, and when the community is in danger, it is up to all the people in the community to fight for those who are menaced, regardless of class or group. . . . You cannot fight the Bolsheviks without fighting the men, women and children in Russia."

Naturally, Hillman came under attack from the conservative elements in his own union, but he was always squarely against the communists in the United States.

Sidney Hillman had an interesting experience with "Golden Rule" Nash in Cincinnati. Nash produced cheap suits and from a small shop employing only a few workers it grew in six years to a company employing 3,000 workers and 2,000 salesmen. Nash claimed that his company gave greater benefits to the workers than any union shop. When Hillman tried to unionize the plant, the workers absolutely refused to go on strike claiming that Nash had done everything for them, including Christmas vacations with pay. Actually, Nash had raised the earnings of the lowest-paid workers 300% when he took over. The company was capitalized at one million dollars and half the stock belonged to the workers. In 1922, Nash increased the wages by 10% and reduced the hours to forty per week. Hillman began a campaign to unionize the plant but it continued to grow in size until it ranked among the largest clothing firms in America.

Hillman finally met this problem by having a conference arranged by the Federal Council of Churches for the discussion of the "Golden Rule" Nash business. The Amalgamated Union was able to show that their pay scale was far below the union wages in Chicago.

The result of the conference was that Nash, at a later meeting, agreed to have all his workers brought into the Amalgamated Union. What had really brought about the transformation was that after Nash had spoken to a large group of manufacturers on the "Golden Rule in Industry," one of them said, "I move we go on record as recognizing this as the greatest scheme to lick unionism that we have ever heard of." This caused Nash to wonder if Hillman was not right, and he decided to unionize all his workers.

Hillman also built cooperative housing for his workers.

Eventually he provided accommodations for 2,536 families with an investment of twenty million dollars.

In the great depression of 1929-1933, Hillman proposed that there should be a five per cent tax on payroll for unemployment insurance. This would mean about one million six hundred thousand dollars annually and would be a tremendous help to the workers in time of depression. Actually, Sidney Hillman proposed this three years before Roosevelt was elected, and such a law was actually enacted.

It is not surprising that during the subsequent New Deal period, he worked in Washington to help make the National Recovery Act effective. In 1934, the Amalgamated was taken into the American Federation of Labor. When the Supreme Court in 1935 declared the National Recovery Act unconstitutional, it precipitated a crisis in the ranks of labor.

In the 1934 and 1935 A.F. of L. conventions, John L. Lewis of the United Mine Workers proposed industrial unionism for the mass industries. Hillman strongly supported his proposal. It was voted down 1,820,000 to 1,090,000.

John L. Lewis then organized the Committee for Industrial Organization which Hillman supported, and it became the C.I.O. In 1937-38, Hillman helped organize the textile workers of America.

During the Roosevelt Administration he became one of the President's most trusted friends and was frequently at the White House in the interests of labor. It is not surprising that he was later called "Statesman of American Labor."

Hillman took an active part in the C.I.O. although John L. Lewis was president. After John L. Lewis had violently opposed the election of President Roosevelt who was nevertheless triumphant, Sidney Hillman was probably responsible for electing Philip Murray to succeed John L. Lewis in the C.I.O.

Hillman was appointed National Defense Commissioner by President Roosevelt. The President told him that he was to have complete responsibility for the labor policy of the whole defense program, and he was to see to it that it was enforced. Hillman himself said, "Every department of government affecting labor in defense (was to be) under my jurisdiction. He gave me the further responsibility for the labor supply, and the whole training of the labor defense industries."

Hillman was responsible for refusing to give the Ford Motor Company an order for 67 million dollars for army trucks even though it was supported by the War Department. He did this because the Ford Company had been ruled in violation of the Wagner Act in nine cases and was strongly opposed to trade unions. But as a result of Hillman's action and in the face of a threatened strike, it agreed to negotiate with the C.I.O.'s United Auto Workers Union. So at last the 140,000 Ford workers joined the ranks of organized labor in 1941. Hillman also helped in the unionization of the Bethlehem Steel Corporation and its 140,000 workers.

When the Office of Production Management was established, Hillman was made Associate Director General by the President. In this position he had the power to review all defense contracts that might cause labor difficulties. It is small wonder that on April 14, 1942, Hillman had a severe heart attack which took him to the hospital. He was then fifty-five years old. After six weeks in the hospital he went back to his old job as President of the Amalgamated Clothing Workers of America.

The Amalgamated had been growing steadily and by 1942 had a membership of 300,000 with locals in thirty-four states. The growing cotton-garment industry in the South was one of the areas where members had been signed up. By this time the cooperative housing projects of the Amalgamated had cost over 20 million dollars. In 1940, the Amalgamated had also started a Life Insurance Association of Chicago which paid death benefits of $500 as well as health and accident insurance to all the workers in the men's and boys' clothing industry. The cost was paid entirely by the employers who contributed 2% of the payroll. By the end of the war, the total of housing, insurance, banking and other cooperative features managed by the union came to roughly 200 million dollars. The union now occupied the space formerly used by Tiffany's in Union Square, New York.

In 1943, it was decided by the C.I.O. to form a Political Action Committee, and Hillman was asked to head the Committee. He tried to get the American Federation of Labor to join, but they refused. He then went on a western tour and succeeded in getting the A.F. of L. unions on the Pacific coast to work with him.

He returned in time for the convention of the C.I.O. in November where Philip Murray paid him a great tribute, saying among other things, that although Hillman was conscripted by the government in the war emergency, he was now "back in the labor movement to put his shoulder to the wheel in building and building this mighty organization."

Hillman made a masterful speech at the convention, stating that the people were at the crossroads of history. "Make up your minds," he said, "that we are either going to get a better world or we are going to be thrown backward. We will not stand still. . . . Make 1944 a year of decision for the common man here and everywhere.

He wanted the American Labor Party to throw its strength behind the Democratic presidential ticket. Dubinsky was opposed. But in the primaries for the American Labor Party Convention, the Hillman ticket won a great victory and he was elected state chairman. The right-wing faction led by Dubinsky and Prof. Counts then formed the American Liberal Party.

Hillman wanted Wallace nominated again for Vice-President, but in the end, Truman was named. Hillman had an extraordinary ability to bring people of diverse points of view together and then get them to work for a common objective. He had the complex task of uniting differing groups both in the political and the labor field. In his political work in the campaign of 1944 for the presidency, the union raised over $700,000.

Governor Dewey attacked Hillman as plotting to subject the United States to a communist dictatorship. Some of the Republican slogans which were used were:

"Sidney Hillman and Earl Browder's communists have registered. Have you?"

"Roosevelt demands all labor questions be cleared with Hillman."

President and Mrs. Roosevelt were even pictured in some of the press as surrounded by the gangsters of Murder, Inc.

Hillman went through all this hysteria and calumny and all the terrible lies that were being hurled at him with equanimity. When friends begged him to bring suit for libel, he said he would meet lies with truth, and the slander of his opponents would boomerang against them. When he was attacked as a Jew he replied: "Red-baiting and Jew-baiting go hand in hand. It is not surprising that Hitler has been calling President Roosevelt a Jew . . . and the native American fascists have been screaming about the Jew Deal and the Hearst-McCormick-Patterson papers' Axis rarely misses an opportunity when discussing the P.A.C. to drag in the fact that I am a Jew and was born in Lithuania. I don't apologize to anybody for it."

When Roosevelt had been overwhelmingly re-elected, the annual convention of the C.I.O. unanimously continued P.A.C. with Hillman as its chairman.

Meanwhile Hillman had been trying to organize a world federation of labor. After the presidential election, Hillman went to London to take part in a world conference of labor bodies. To show how courageous Hillman was—when his doctors advised him to safeguard his health and not go to London, he replied, "I know this may shorten my life, but I have to make up my mind whether to live ten years longer as an invalid or do what I can do now."

The preliminary World Trade Union Conference meeting in December 1944 included representatives of only Britain, Russia, and the United States. Hillman won approval for a plan for a permanent world labor organization to be presented to a second conference. In February 1945, he headed the delegation to a second overseas conference which was attended by trade-union representatives from fifty-three nations. Through Hillman's efforts the Russians agreed to accept a far smaller proportion of votes than their trade-union membership would have allowed, and the conference was a success. Thus Hillman was to no small degree responsible for the establishment of the World Federation of Trade-Unions (W.F.T.U.).

During World War II, Hillman's mother and sister were brutally executed by the Nazis when they seized Lithuania.

Speaking of the Jews in Germany he said, "There is only one place they want to go to, and that is Palestine. . . . And I say that none has the moral right to stop them."

As a Jew Hillman had been very active in giving aid to the Jews who were being exterminated by Hitler and in seeking the establishment of a Jewish state in Palestine. He secured the adoption by the World Federation of Trade-Unions of a resolution that a Jewish state be established in Palestine. Before his death he was to see the establishment of the State of Israel.

When the State Department became friendly with Generalissimo Franco, Hillman strongly opposed the move and sent the following telegram to President Truman: "World War II started in Spain when Nazi Germany and Fascist Italy replaced the legal government with the illegal Nazi regime led by Franco. Franco's status as enemy power and satellite of Mussolini was recognized by his exclusion from the U.N. at San Francisco and Potsdam. . . . Urge you request . . . that allied nations complete eradication of Nazis by withdrawing recognition from Franco and allowing Spain to reinstate its own legal democratic government." Unfortunately, his advice was not followed.

The World Federation of Trade-Unions held its first session on October 3, 1945 with over 500 delegates representing 56 countries and 70 million union members. Sir Walter Citrine was elected President and Hillman, one of the Vice-Presidents. One action of the conference was for a small committee including Hillman to visit Germany to observe the process of denazification and to investigate what could be done to build a free German labor movement. Due to Hillman's vigorous work the W.F.T.U. won semiofficial recognition from the U.N. General Assembly.

On January 31, 1946, Hillman left the States to visit

the terrible Nazi concentration camps, observe conditions in all the military occupation zones, and attend the Nuremburg trials of war criminals.

With all that Hillman was doing it was not surprising that he suffered a second heart atttack when he returned to the United States in March, 1946. In spite of this he attended the Fifteenth Convention of the Amalgamated Clothing Workers on May 6th and delivered one of the major addresses.

He said that for the first time in fifteen years, the world was free from the threat of fascism and "today our first concern is the winning of the peace." He pleaded that the United States, Russia, and Great Britain work together. He wisely stated, "But if the unity of the Big Three fails, then I am afraid . . . the U.N. will become no more than an area for the play of power politics." He ended his address with these words: "My friends, we have accomplished much. But we cannot rest on our laurels. This is a time when everything is at stake. There is no middle way. This is either going to be a free world or a world where only slaves will live."

As the convention closed Hillman spoke these final words:

"It is within the power of America to provide for our people conditions beyond the dreams of generations past. Not only do we have a tremendous productivity, but now is the time when we can open the door to the atomic age. This earth can be made a place where men and women can walk together in peace and friendship and enjoy all that this world can provide for; but we must see to it that the power of government is placed at the service of the people instead of in the control of the privileged few, selfish, greedy people who do not accept the right of the common man and do not understand what democracy means. . . . Our program is not a class program. Ours is not a selfish program. Ours is a program for all America.

"We want a better America, an America that will give its citizens, first of all, a higher and higher standard of living, so that no child will cry for food in the midst of plenty. We want to have an America where the inventions of science will be at the disposal of every American family, not merely for the few who can afford them. An America that will have no sense of insecurity and which will make it possible for all the groups to live in friendship and to be real neighbors; an America that will carry on its great mission of helping other countries to help themselves, thinking not in terms of exploitation, but of creating plenty abroad so we can all enjoy it here."

Shortly after the convention, Hillman had a third heart attack and in little more than a month, on July 10, 1946, he was dead.

Sidney Hillman was one of the great leaders of the labor movement. His sincerity, his devotion, his unflagging zeal to work for the common good made his life shine out like a beacon light. He had devoted his life day in and day out to winning justice for the workers. No task was too hard, no hours were to long for him when he was striving for righteousness and the welfare of all.

Won't you who are reading these words take a moment to contrast your own life with his? What lessons can you learn? Can you do more than you have done to follow in the footsteps of one who gave his life that others might have abundance and happiness?

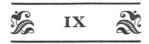

IX

WALTER REUTHER

WALTER REUTHER IS one of the most dynamic labor leaders in America today. Whenever I meet him I am inspired by what he has accomplished. His life spells the advances that labor has been making in the past decades. The basic purpose of Walter Reuther is well summed up in his closing address to the Congress of Industrial Organizations on December 2, 1955: "There is no greater calling than to serve your brothers. There is no greater contribution than to help the weak. There is no greater satisfaction than to have done it well."

Walter Reuther was born in Wheeling, West Virginia, on September 1, 1907. His father was an international representative of the Brewery Workers Union and already President of the Central Trades and Labor Assembly in Wheeling, West Virginia, when he was twenty-three years old. Reuther learned from his father the philosophy of trade-unionism, the struggles, the hopes, the aspirations of working people. Reuther has said; "I was raised in the kind of trade-union atmosphere that said to me when I was a boy that a trade-union movement based upon principles of pure and simple trade unionism was not enough. In a free and interdependent society, labor can make progress only to the extent that it helps to provide leadership in solving the problems of all the people."

He served as an apprentice tool and die maker in the

Wheeling Steel Corp. in 1924. He studied three years at Wayne University in Detroit, and while he did not graduate, his grades were excellent. From 1927 to 1932, he was employed by Briggs Manufacturing Co., General Motors Corp., and the Ford Motor Co. in Detroit. He became a foreman in the Ford Motor Co. in 1931. He probably could have stayed on and become an executive, but he was more interested in serving the interests of the workers.

Consequently, from 1932 to 1935, he traveled by bicycle through Europe, the Soviet Union, and the Orient, observing auto plants and machine shops. He described his experience in the Soviet Union as follows: "I worked in the Soviet Union as a worker in the Gorki automobile plant for eighteen months, and as a worker, not a tourist, I traveled over eighteen thousand miles throughout the Soviet Union including the Soviet Republics of Central Asia and Siberia. I worked with and I know and learned to love the Russian people. They share the same hopes, the same aspirations, and they dream the same dreams as other people. They have made great progress in developing an industrial nation. No one can deny the fact that the people of the Soviet Union have gained a measure of economic progress and economic security. But no one who has lived and worked with the people of the Soviet Union can deny the harsh fact that while they have won more bread, they have not won more freedom."

He concludes: "The communist way in the Soviet Union or in the Chinese People's Republic inevitably subordinates the worth and the value of the individual."

In 1935, Reuther returned to America and helped organize the automobile workers. He established and became President of Local 174 of the United Automobile Workers of the C.I.O. By 1939 he was Director of the General

Motors Division of the union. In 1946, he became President of the U.A.W. and in 1952, President of the C.I.O.

When the A.F. of L. and C.I.O. were merged in 1955, Reuther became Vice-President and has retained this office ever since. Of course he continues to serve as President of the U.A.W. He is also Vice-President of the International Confederation of Free Trade-Unions.

Reuther has taken on a great many outside posts. He was a member of the Labor Management Policy Committee of the War Manpower Commission and a member of the Labor Management Policy Committee of the Labor Production Division of W.P.B. Today he is a member of the Board of Trustees of Roosevelt College in Chicago and of the President's Advisory Committee on Labor-Management Relations.

Long ago Reuther advocated the Peace Corps which has only recently been realized. He early took a stand against the communists in the labor movement and succeeded in driving them out of the U.A.W. and C.I.O. He has been prophetic in pointing out the weaknesses in American industry. For instance, as far back as 1940, he said that no industry in the world has the tremendous unused productive capacity of the American automobile industry. To quote his exact words: "During the automotive year ending August, 1940, Nash used only 17 percent of its productive capacity; Dodge used 36½ percent. Nash, working at maximum capacity, could have manufactured its total output for the twelve months in 49½ working days." He went on to say that Chevrolet was using only 50 percent of its total capacity. He declared that Fisher Body Plant No. 23 which in 1931 employed 4,800 tool and diemakers used only 175 in December, 1940, and these were on a reduced work week. He also showed how hundreds of thousands of square feet of floor space were not being used for production in many plants.

Reuther proposed back in 1945 that these idle facilities could be used in peace time. He said, "We have to mobilize for peace the resourcefulness and technical know-how which put the B-29 in the skies over Tokyo and sent the atomic bomb crashing into Hiroshima,—and we can wipe out the slums and the substandard housing, both rural and urban, which sap the health and dignity of millions of American families."

He advocated a guaranteed annual wage and said, "This represents a challenge to management to sponsor the greatest 'back to work' movement in the history of labor relations. . . . If we fail, our epitaph will be simply stated: we had the ingenuity to unlock the secrets of the universe for the purposes of destruction, but we lacked the courage and imagination to work together in the creative pursuits of peace."

Walter Reuther stated vigorously and clearly what we must do "to beat the communists." The main way, he said, was "the neverending task of making democracy work, keeping it alive, and fighting against injustice." He said, "Communism is in perpetual war with what democracy preaches, for it cannot abide the sanctity of the individual or the interplay of honest differences. But communism breeds on and exploits the lapses of the democratic conscience. . . . It is the task of democrats to bridge the gap between preachment and practice; we must wipe out the double standards in America and in the world. . . . Communism breeds on hunger, poverty, human insecurity. The Catholic peasants of Italy have never read Marx or Lenin. But in desperation they will vote communist for land and bread if Italian democrats fail them."

Reuther made clear why he favored higher wages for the workers. In 1949, he said, "Profits have gone up three times as fast as wages and salaries." He noted the fact that in the automobile industry, eight companies including Ford had profits 51% higher than in 1947.

He cited the compensation of the executives. For instance, C. E. Wilson of General Motors got $516,000 in salary and bonus in 1948. He was making $258 an hour. Yet General Motors agreed to give him $25,000 a year when he retired. The top seven executives in General Motors had salaries averaging $46,799 in 1948. Reuther believed that the workers who received low wages should have security when they were too old to work and also a health and medical plan.

Reuther believed the corporations gave their high-paid officials fat pensions when they didn't need them while they denied pensions to working people who did need them.

When he accepted the presidency of the C.I.O. in 1952, he said in his address: "We must fight the forces of monopoly and scarcity in their opposition to the expansion of our productive capacity and the full development of our productive resources. . . . The real measurement of the greatness of a civilization is its ability to demonstrate the sense of social and moral responsibility needed to translate material values into human values, technological progress into human progress, human happiness, and human dignity."

In this same address he stated again what he believed about meeting the communist threat. "There is a revolution going on in the world. The communists didn't start the revolution. It is a revolution of hungry men to get the wrinkles out of their empty bellies. It is a revolution of people who have been exploited by imperialism and who are trying to throw off the shackles of imperialism and colonialism and who want to march forward in freedom and independence. It is a struggle of the have-nots to get something for themselves. The communists didn't start it. They are riding its back. What we have to do is to answer the communist propaganda not with slogans; we must expose the hypocrisy of communist propaganda which offers the hungry and desperate people the promise of economic security with a price tag.

"We need to answer the reactionaries in Wall Street who play the other side of that communist record. The communists would have people trade freedom for bread and the reactionaries would have you believe that if you want to be free you have to be economically insecure. And we say to the communists and the reactionaries, You are both wrong. In the world that we are trying to help build, people can have both bread and freedom."

He went on to say: "This struggle in the world between freedom and tyranny, between democracy and communism, is a struggle for men's minds and their hearts and their loyalties. It cannot be won on the battlefields. It can only be won on the economic and social field in the struggle for human justice. . . . One third of the people of the world are living on less than a dollar a week, and that is why they are the easy victims of communist propaganda. . . . I believe that history will prove. . . . that the more young Americans we send abroad with medical kits and slide rules and textbooks as technical missionaries to work on the social and economic fronts, the fewer American boys we will need to send with guns and tanks and planes to fight on the battle fronts."

His conclusion was something that should ring around America. "You can get people marching and sacrificing and fighting for the negative ends of war, and yet we haven't found the way to mobilize that spiritual power for the positive ends of peace."

Speaking at the Fifteenth Convention of the C.I.O. in Cleveland on March 7, 1955, Reuther demanded a guaranteed annual wage. He said that if in 1954 the United States had utilized its manpower and economic resources, it could have produced 40 billion dollars more wealth. He said General Motors made 1,645 million dollars but "the factory workers of Michigan alone in one year because of unemployment lost 640 million dollars." This meant that the workers could not buy that amount of goods and services and consequently the prosperity of the country was reduced by that extent.

Reuther analyzed the salary of Mr. Curtice, President of the General Motors Corporation, on an hourly basis. He believed Mr. Curtice was paid $329 an hour. He said it would take the average General Motors worker one hundred fifty years to earn what Mr. Curtice received in one year. He maintained that the Chairman of the Board of General Motors received an hourly income of $2,178 if you included what he received on his stock.

Because of these facts Reuther held that the workers who received so little should at least be guaranteed an annual wage and that since automation "destroys unskilled jobs and creates skilled jobs," the workers should be retrained for the new jobs. Said Reuther, "If the result of automation is that a large number of workers in a plant have to learn new skills, I believe it is just as reasonable to expect the employer to pay the cost of retraining, including the payment of wages during the retraining period, as it is that he should pay the cost of building the new plant or installing new equipment."

As far back as 1956 Reuther pleaded for the use of atomic power for peace. "In the cold war, in freedom's struggle against the forces of communist tyranny, in the struggle for the hearts and minds of men, speed, all possible speed in harnessing the atom to man's peacetime needs can be decisive.

"Access to low-cost nuclear power may prove the key to the economic development of backward areas and make possible the liberation of millions of people from poverty, hunger, ignorance, and disease. America's leadership is essential if we are to block the communists in their efforts to forge poverty into power.

"Our success in harnessing the atom to lift the burden of poverty and disease from hundreds of millions of the world's people living in hunger and ill-health would establish America in a position of moral leadership against which communist propaganda would be impotent.

"Harnessing of the atom for peaceful purposes will give us the tools with which to wage freedom's most effective propaganda to these people,—the propaganda of the democratic deed."

Reuther also pleaded for federal aid to education. He said, "The crisis in the world is not economic, military, or political; essentially it is a moral crisis. It is a reflection of man's growing inhumanity to man. . . . This growing lag between our know-how in the physical sciences and our failure to make comparable progress in learning to know and understand and work with people, confronts us with a very serious dilemma . . . Somehow, people arrived at the idea that you can stop communism with guns. Nothing could be more tragic than for America to believe that."

He quoted Dr. James R. Killian, Jr., President of the Massachusetts Institute of Technology, as recognizing that

Russia has outstripped the United States in the output of scientists and engineers. He cited the fact that in 1955, American universities and colleges graduated 27,000 engineers and scientists while the Soviets graduated 34,000; also that Russia had three times as many students in the field of engineering and the physical sciences as the United States and was doing as qualitative a job in their training. Actually Reuther believes they are doing a better job. The average graduate of a Soviet engineering school knows as much as a United States graduate with a Master's degree.

"In the United States," Reuther said, "the average sweeper in the automobile factory under contract with my union, the man on the lowest rung of the wage ladder, last year made more money than fifty percent of the elementary school teachers in America." Later he said, "I think it is nothing short of insanity to train people and then to have tremendous shortages in the field of their specialized training, because we dumped them into the Army for two years of boot training. The Russians are not doing it, but we are."

Reuther suggested that Congress establish a broad and comprehensive system of federal scholarships to be awarded to students on a competitive basis and that such students be obligated to serve wherever there was a teacher shortage, or a peacetime atomic program for a period of one year longer than their normal military service from which they would be excused. He also indicated that today we are losing about 60 percent of our top high school students who cannot go to college.

It seems to me that Reuther again expressed his far-sighted moral convictions when he addressed the Indian Council on World Affairs at New Delhi on April 5, 1955. He there stated: "Neither peace nor freedom can be made

secure in a world of nuclear giants and moral pigmies. . . .
The greater dilemma in the world grows out of the developing moral and cultural lag between man's moral progress
in the physical sciences and his lack of comparable progress
in the human and social sciences."

He went on to say that he believed that freedom's struggle in Asia will be won primarily in the rice fields and not
in the battlefields.

He proposed that the United Nations establish a world
fund for *peace, prosperity* and *progress* and that the
United States contribute to this fund a sum equal to 2%
of the gross national product for a period of twenty-five
years. This fund would be used to help the people of the
less advanced nations of the world to develop their economic resources and raise their standards of living, health,
and education. He wanted the United States to give regardless of what any other nation did; however, the Soviet
Union should be urged to give a similar amount. The
funds would be administered by the United Nations. The
United States would agree to share its food surplus with
the countries suffering from acute shortages. A scholarship
program would be created for training engineers, doctors,
and technicians who could help in these countries. Reuther
proposed that United States economic aid be made available to every free and independent nation without any
political strings whatever.

In Reuther's speech in India, he also came out strongly
in favor of the "freedom riders" in the Southern states of
the United States and in favor of integration in the schools.

When Reuther was summoned before the Senate Sub-
committee on Privileges and Elections on October 9, 1956,
he defended the right of labor to make campaign contribu-
tions in time of elections. He pointed out that in the

United States, four families had actually contributed more in the presidential election of 1952 than one and a half million members of the Automobile Workers Union. He therefore demolished the arguments that unions should not contribute to political campaigns. Senator Gore said at the end of the hearing: "It seems to me that there is a basic threat to popular government, when roughly one percent of the people finance 95 to 98 percent of our political campaigns. We need to reform our system." Reuther was willing to have a limitation on what one man could donate to a political campaign.

He is unalterably opposed, as one would expect, to racketeering and corruption in the labor movement. He says, "There should be no room for either crooks or communists in the leadership of our kind of free labor movement."

However, he is also strongly opposed to corruption in management. He says, "Corrupt managements would rather pay a bribe to a crooked labor leader than to pay a living wage to the workers represented by that crooked labor leader. I say that an employer who bribes a labor leader is as morally guilty as the crook who took the bribe."

Reuther is also absolutely opposed to any discrimination in race relations. He tells of Bishop Oxnam's remark that there is a lot of noble talk about the brotherhood of man, but some of the people who mouth the words "keep the hood and drop the brother" in action. Because of Reuther's activities, four Negroes were elected to important positions in Detroit. He attacked Senator Eastland of the House Un-American Activities Committee saying, "He doesn't know anything about what makes a communist. What he does not understand are the great social, dynamic forces sweeping the world. . . . This is a struggle for the hearts and minds of people."

His reply to an attack against him in a leaflet entitled, "Behind the Plot to Sovietize the South," was: "I want to say to the people who put out this kind of literary trash that the NAACP, the A.F. of L.-C.I.O., and all the good people who are joined together in the fight for civil rights do more to fight the communists in one week than all these people do in their whole lives put together."

Repeatedly he has attacked the automobile companies for collusion in fixing prices. He pointed out that in the first nine months of 1955, General Motors profits represented a return of 36.5 percent after all taxes had been paid. Ford's profits were 26.1 percent after taxes and Chrysler's, 12.2 percent after taxes.

In 1959, Walter Reuther made a statement to the Joint Congressional Economic Committee. He cited the 1957 Bureau of the Census figures which show that almost 25 percent of American families have incomes below three thousand dollars. He went on to say that 2.8 million families had incomes below one thousand dollars and there were 6.5 million families with incomes below $2,000. He believed that all this was unnecessary; it merely represented "a continuation of drift and the waste of idle manpower and productive capacity." He quoted Secretary of State Dulles, speaking to the U.S. Chamber of Commerce in 1958, as saying: "Whereas Soviet gross national product was about 33 percent that of the U.S. in 1950 . . . by 1962 it may be about 50 percent of our own. This means that the Soviet economy has been growing and is expected to continue to grow through 1962 at a rate roughly twice that of the economy of the United States."

This also means that the Soviet Union will eventually catch up and surpass us.

Reuther proposed the following remedies:

1. Federal assistance for economically distressed communities.

2. Minimum federal standards for unemployment insurance.

3. Congressional action to provide assistance to municipalities for water, gas, sewer, and other facilities.

4. Defense and other government contracts placed in distressed areas with serious unemployment.

5. A minimum wage of $1.25 an hour and extension of the law to millions of workers in retail and wholesale trades.

6. Increased Social Security benefits and medical aid for the aged.

7. A government Commission set up to devise social and economic programs to cushion dislocations from automation.

8. Progressive reduction of the work week to prevent unemployment.

9. Federal aid for school construction and educational scholarships.

10. A national housing program to provide good homes in decent neighborhoods for all American families.

11. Hospital and highway programs.

In addition Reuther urged adequate defence, economic and technical aid for people emerging from colonialism, increased wages and salaries to expand consumer buying power, a policy of rapid economic growth to prevent unemployment, increased international trade, and the establishment of international fair labor standards and fair employment practices for minority groups at home.

Reuther believed that the cost of these programs could be met and that 9 billion dollars in additional revenue could be secured by closing current loopholes in the tax structure.

In his address to the Berlin Freedom Rally in May 1959, Reuther showed his prophetic insight. "I can say in truthfulness that the only war in which the American people wish to engage is the war against poverty, hunger, ignorance, and disease. . . . This is our goal. A world of peace, freedom, and social justice for all people everywhere. . . . Together we shall build a world of peace, freedom, security, social justice, and brotherhood."

In September 1959, he and other labor leaders met Khrushchev in the United States. Khrushchev got angry at some of the questions and called Reuther a "capitalist lackey." Reuther responded by saying, "Wall Street says I am an agent of Moscow, and Moscow says I am an agent of Wall Street."

While Reuther is bitterly opposed to the conservatism of Barry Goldwater and claims that if we translated his book, *The Conscience of a Conservative,* into governmental action, "the communists would take over the world in the next five years." On the other hand he is just as much opposed to every corrupt leader in the labor movement.

Walter Reuther is one of the outstanding prophetic voices in the American labor movement and the American people would do well to heed carefully what he says. His basic theory is that we must achieve justice, health, education and prosperity for American society and for world freedom.

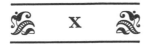

X

FRANKLIN DELANO ROOSEVELT

I DID NOT KNOW President Roosevelt very well. On one occasion I stayed overnight at the White House and had some long talks with him, and showed moving pictures I had taken in Russia. He said they were the best pictures he had ever seen of Russia. Like every citizen, I watched his career and I came to admire him more and more. Those who are critical today should ask themselves, "How do your tasks and achievements make for righteousness? Are *you* helping to make the world any better?"

Franklin Roosevelt definitely did. He overcame obstacles and devoted his time and efforts to the common good as he saw it.

He was born January 30, 1882, in Hyde Park and was named after his mother's favorite uncle. As a child he had French and German governesses who took care of him. Later, private tutors started his education. Few children in the United States enjoyed the many privileges that were his. In the summer, the family went to Maine and often took trips abroad. His first trip was when he was only three years old. At seven, Franklin had his own pony. One of his hobbies was collecting birds, and he had a wonderful collection mounted by himself.

From the ages of seven to fifteen he was taken abroad each summer. He came to know France, England, and Germany firsthand. He actually toured Germany and

Switzerland by bicycle with a tutor for two summers. The tradition of service was strong in the family. They felt their obligations toward the unfortunate and impressed them upon the son. Therefore, Franklin grew up with a sympathy for the underprivileged and a resentment against the injustice that caused their condition.

He was sent at fourteen to Groton School where he became an excellent debater. He would have run away at sixteen and entered the Navy in the Spanish-American War but fortunately came down with measles instead.

He entered Harvard in 1900. He campaigned for William Jennings Bryan that year despite the fact that his beloved uncle "Ted" was running for Vice-President along with McKinley.

That same year, his father died. Franklin fell in love with Eleanor Roosevelt, both of whose parents had died. By 1903 he was elected president of the *Harvard Crimson,* and the same year became engaged to Eleanor. They were married the next year. He finished Harvard in three years but with an average scholastic record. He stayed on at the university for studies in government, history, and international law. He next went to Columbia Law School and then in 1910 was a delegate to the Democratic State Convention.

Whenever I saw him, Roosevelt made me feel at home. He had a magnetic personality which attracted those who met him. Watching him closely over the years, I felt that he wanted to do the things that would be approved in the final judgment of history. I became convinced that he was deeply religious and had respect for every religious faith. He himself was Episcopalian and a Senior Warden at St. James Church in Hyde Park. As Mrs. Roosevelt said, he had a very simple religion: "He believed in God and in His guidance . . . he actually felt he could ask God for His guidance and receive it." It is interesting that when Roosevelt was later negotiating with Stalin, he insisted that any religious group in the Soviet Union which had enough members should be permitted to have a pastor or a priest. The Russians finally agreed to this.

Mrs. Roosevelt was also a remarkable person in her own right. She had rare intelligence, interest in social problems, a sense of humor, and great ability in writing and speaking.

In 1918, Roosevelt was elected to the New York Legislature as State Senator. Next he set out to defeat Billy Sheehan who was running for United States Senator. He incurred the enmity of the bosses in Tammany Hall, but Sheehan was defeated. Later, he formed a committee to help elect Woodrow Wilson as President, and in this he was also successful.

When Woodrow Wilson became President, Roosevelt was appointed Assistant Secretary of the Navy. He worked hard in this post and after a visit to France, came down with double pneumonia. On one trip from Europe, he came back with President Wilson who had the draft of the League of Nations with him. Roosevelt became a strong advocate of the League.

At thirty-eight Franklin was nominated for Vice-President on the Democratic ticket with James W. Cox of Ohio but was defeated in the election by the Republican Warren G. Harding who captured the presidency. In the campaign, Roosevelt averaged more than ten speeches a day and shook hands with a million people. In his acceptance speech for the nomination, he uttered words which forecast his later program:

"The Democratic Party offers a larger life for our country, a richer destiny for our people. . . .

"Our opposition is to the things which once existed, in order that they may never return. . . .

"We oppose money in politics; we oppose the private
control of national finances; we oppose the treating of
human beings as commodities; we oppose the saloon-
bossed city; we oppose starvation wages; we oppose rule
by groups or cliques."

The next year he contracted polio but in spite of this
was elected Governor of New York in 1928. Roosevelt
treated his infantile paralysis by going to Warm Springs.
As a result he gave his money, time, and interest to the
Foundation there, and almost a million dollars was raised
to help carry on the work for the victims of paralysis.

Roosevelt was a great reader of biography and history.
For recreation he did crossword puzzles, played cards, and
collected stamps. Before becoming a polio victim, he had
loved horseback riding. And of course he always loved
swimming.

As governor he fought against unjust rates for the public
utilities and championed an old-age-pension law for needy
persons over seventy, an eight-hour day on public works,
and additional farm relief, among other things. William
Green, President of the American Federation of Labor,
became an ardent supporter of his. In my conversations
with Roosevelt he was always sympathetic to labor. He
felt that they should have just as much justice and power as
capital.

He was elected to the governorship for a second term by
a record vote. He had ingratiated himself with the Catho-
lics by supporting Alfred E. Smith. As for the Jews, he had
Herbert H. Lehman as lieutenant governor, Julius Cohen
as a member of his power commission, and Henry Morgenthau, Jr. as chairman of his agricultural advisory commission. He became stronger and stronger among the Democratic party leaders.

In 1932 he was nominated for the presidency and won the election, carrying forty-two out of forty-eight states. The danger of war was very real, and in his acceptance speech he said, ". . . This is preeminently the time to speak the truth, the whole truth, frankly and boldly. Nor need we shrink from honestly facing conditions in our country today. This great nation will endure as it has endured, will revive and prosper. So, first of all, let me assert my firm belief that the only thing that we have to fear is fear itself. Nameless, unreasoning, unjustified terror which paralyzes needed efforts to convert retreat into advance. . . . The money changers have fled from their high seats in the temple of our civilization. We may now restore that temple to the ancient truths. The measure of the restoration lies in the extent to which we apply social values more noble than mere monetary profit."

Naturally, Roosevelt was viciously attacked in his political campaigns. Mrs. Roosevelt said that there was hardly a campaign where "scurrilous things were not said" about him. But he adhered to his objective "to help make life better for the average man, woman, and child."

The next few years were the golden age of the New Deal. It helped labor organize and protected it from exploitation. It assisted farmers by raising the prices they received; provided more security for the family, for the aged, and sick; and blocked waste in the farm lands, mines, and forests.

Roosevelt was outstandingly liberal in his approach to the nation's problems. In March, 1930, he said: "Let us not forget that there can be an aristocracy of special classes or commercial interests which is utterly incompatible with a real democracy. . . ." In speaking to the American Legion the same year he stated: "These are the wars where we who believe in progress, who believe in bettering the safety, the security, and happiness of every individual in the nation, move forward in perpetual assault on the forces of conservatism, of selfishness, of greed, and of entrenched tradition which belongs to a past generation rather than to this twentieth century."

In April, 1932: "These unhappy times call for the building of plans that rest upon the forgotten, the unorganized, but the indispensable units of economic power . . . that build from the bottom up and not from the top down, that put their faith once more in the forgotten man at the bottom of the economic pyramid. . . . Here should be an objective of government itself, to provide at least as much assistance to the little fellow as it is now giving to the large banks and corporations."

Roosevelt tried to carry out these principles during his years in the White House. He was frequently charged with being socialistic, but history has rendered the verdict that he served the interests of all the people and the welfare of the United States.

In 1936, Roosevelt ran against Governor Landon of Kansas for the presidency and again won. He spoke out with great fearlessness as illustrated by these extracts from one of his addresses:

> . . . From out of this modern civilization, economic royalists carved new dynasties . . . the whole structure of modern life was impressed into this royal service.
>
> There was no place among this royalty for the many thousands of small business men and merchants who sought to make a worthy use of the American system of initiative and profit. . . .
>
> The privileged princes of these new economic dynasties, thirsting for power, reached out for control of

government itself. They created a new despotism and wrapped it in robes of legal sanction. . .

Against economic tyranny such as this, the American citizen could appeal only to the organized power of government. The collapse of 1929 showed up the despotism for what it was.

Is it any wonder that Roosevelt carried all but two states, Maine and Vermont? During this term he was to face the problems of World War II. Italy surrendered unconditionally on September 8, 1943. Roosevelt made arrangements for a conference with Churchill and Stalin in Teheran. President Roosevelt used the Russian Embassy as his guest house. The Russians did everything possible to make his stay there delightful. Roosevelt agreed that all peace measures would have to depend on united action by England, Russia, and the United States. Therefore, any one of the three could exercise a veto. As a result of this conference it was agreed that an invasion through France should start on the first of May. The declaration signed on December 1, 1943 by Churchill, Roosevelt, and Stalin said, among other things: "We recognize fully the supreme responsibility resting upon us and all the nations to make a peace which will command good will from the overwhelming masses of the peoples of the world and banish the scourge and terror of war for many generations . . .

"We came here with hope and determination. We leave here friends in fact, in spirit, and in purpose."

Roosevelt felt that the world would gradually become more socialistic as time went on. Mrs. Roosevelt made this comment: "Stalin, Churchill and Roosevelt, in their very different ways, were extraordinarily good people to have been thrown together to achieve success in this war. All of them, without question, led their people and gave so unstintedly of their own strength that they inspired confidence and respect."[1]

Roosevelt was nominated for the presidency again in 1944 and won the election for the fourth time. He was inaugurated on January 20, 1945 and two days later left for a conference in Yalta, U.S.S.R. Roosevelt always felt grateful to the Soviet Union for having kept so many of the German army divisions occupied on the eastern front. While the Yalta conference was in progress, the Soviet armies were driving the Germans back and destroying them.

It was agreed at Yalta that Germany should never again be rearmed. All three concurred: "It is our inflexible purpose to destroy German militarism and Nazism and to ensure that Germany will never again be able to disturb the peace of the world. We are determined to disarm and disband all German armed forces; break up for all time the German general staff that has repeatedly contrived the resurgence of German militarism; remove or destroy all German military equipment; eliminate or control all German industry that could be used for military production." (From the official report of the Crimea Conference) Elliott Roosevelt, in his book describing the conference, stated that it was not the fault of the Soviet Union that these stringent terms were not lived up to.

Long before the Nazi collapse, the foreign ministers and the war ministers of the Big Three circulated draft memoranda of what the surrender terms should be. The Soviet Union sent a copy to Marshal Zhukov, but none was sent to General Eisenhower. Elliott Roosevelt said: "In fact the surrender terms he used were drawn up by his chief

[1] Eleanor Roosevelt, *This I Remember*. (New York, Harper and Brothers, 1949), p. 316.

of staff, General Beedle Smith, for the reason that he knew of no existing document." In explaining the resultant deterioration of relationships with the Soviet Union, Elliott Roosevelt stated: "In my effort to get back to first and underlying causes for our critical present, I note only that it was the United States and Great Britain who first shook the mailed fist, who first abrogated the collective decisions."[2]

Roosevelt was determined to have frequent meetings of the Big Three. Unfortunately, on April 12, 1945 President Roosevelt died. The cold war was soon resumed, and the United States did not live up to all the agreements made at Yalta.

Here we have the life of a great American. His private secretary, Grace Tully, said he was "a man of straightforward simplicity, courage, passion and honesty." He gave everything he had to the cause of freedom and justice. He refused to be bought by the men of great wealth. He constantly thought of the welfare of the common people. In spite of polio and physical disabilities, he devoted himself to what he believed was right and in the interest of the people. Had he lived longer, the terrible animosities between East and West would not have grown to the point where they threaten to precipitate World War III.

What are you doing with your life to make it serve the common good, as Roosevelt tried to do?

[2] Elliott Roosevelt, *As He Saw It*. (New York, Duell, Sloan & Pearce).

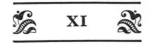

XI

STEPHEN S. WISE

STEPHEN WISE WAS a wonderful man. Every contact I had with him was inspiring and reinforced my esteem and affection for him. Although I was a Christian minister he invited me to speak in the Free Synagogue. Later he invited me to accompany him to Israel. I came to feel that he was one of the great religious leaders of his time.

Dr. Wise was born in Budapest, Hungary, on March 17, 1874. His father and grandfather were both rabbis. His father came to America with the family in 1875 and served as rabbi of Temple Rodeph Sholom in New York.

Stephen attended public school and won many prizes. Later he went to City College and then Columbia University. He graduated with honors in 1892. From his earliest youth he had determined to enter the ministry so immediately after his graduation from Columbia he went abroad and was ordained in Vienna under Chief Rabbi Jellinek. Upon his return to the United States he became the assistant to Rabbi Jacobs at Temple B'nai Jeshrun and when Jacobs died became the Chief Rabbi at 23 years of age.

In 1898 Stephen Wise met Louise Waterman, and two years later they were married. Just before his marriage, he had accepted a call to Temple Bethel in Portland, Oregon. He felt that he needed a wider acquaintance with the United States than just New York City.

There he became active in seeking good government

and in 1903 was appointed Commissioner of Child Labor for the State of Oregon. While in Oregon, Rabbi Wise accepted invitations from Christian ministers to preach in their churches and interpret the Jewish faith to them. He had a life contract at a very high salary, but he longed to start a synagogue in New York which would have a free pulpit and where the pews would be open to rich and poor alike and where he could tackle the social problems of the city as well as its religious needs.

Temple Emanuel-El of New York, known as the Cathedral Synagogue, wanted Rabbi Wise, but he insisted that if he came, the pulpit must be entirely free for him to speak the truth as he saw it. When the Board asked him what he meant by "free" this was his reply:

> Mr. Moses, it is rumored that your nephew, Mr. Herman, is to be a Tammany Hall candidate for a Supreme Court judgeship. I would, if I were Emanuel-El's rabbi, oppose his candidacy in and out of my pulpit. Mr. Guggenheim, as a member of the Child Labor Commission of the State of Oregon, I must say to you that, if it ever came to be known that children were being employed in your mines, I would cry out against such wrong. Mr. Marshall, the press stated that you and your firm are to be counsel for Mr. Hyde of the Equitable Life Assurance Society. That may or may not be true, but knowing that Charles Evans Hughes' investigation of insurance companies in New York has been a very great service, I would in and out of my pulpit speak in condemnation of the crimes committed by the insurance thieves.

Rabbi Wise was not appointed to the Cathedral Synagogue.

His devotion to his principles was demonstrated when

he organized the Free Synagogue in New York with less than fifty members in April 1907, and refused to accept any salary the first year. All he took the second year was three thousand dollars.

At first he had some hostility from temple and synagogue groups. One of the leading rabbis of New York when attacking him described the Free Synagogue as "a hall with an orator and audience and a pitcher of ice water."

Actually Dr. Wise started his services in the Hudson Theatre, then went to the Universalist Church of Our Father and from 1910 to 1940 occupied Carnegie Hall.

Stephen Wise said: "One of the deepest satisfactions of my life has been to see that the Jewish pulpit is become free, that is to say as free as the men who stand in it will it to be, and that many younger men in the Christian ministry have generously acknowledged that they owe the freedom of their pulpits in part to the battle I once waged when I declared that a pulpit that is not free is without moral and spiritual meaning."

Rabbi Wise also started the Social Service Division of the Synagogue which did work among Jewish patients at Bellevue Hospital and later Lebanon and Montefiore. A free Synagogue branch on the East Side was set up with the encouragement and support of the Henry Street Settlement. Meetings were held Sunday evening, and they also had a religious school. This brought religious work into an underprivileged community of the city.

Henry Morgenthau, Sr., was for a number of years the helpful and generous president of the synagogue, but eventually he became an anti-Zionist and broke with the Free Synagogue on that issue.

Stephen Wise had long had an interest in Palestine. The successor to his grandfather as Chief Rabbi in Hungary was dragged away to die by his Nazi captors in 1945. His father's mother refused to come to the United States to live with the Wise family, because she wanted to go to Palestine. She wrote: "I go not to live there but to die there. There I wish to pray and there to die, to be laid to rest amid the sacred dust of Jerusalem; to be buried on the slope facing the Holy of Holies."

Stephen Wise first went to Palestine with his wife in 1913. Although he carried a letter from President Wilson, the authorities would permit him to remain only a few weeks in the country. The Mayor of Tel Aviv gave him some delicious oranges, saying he hoped that Jewish Palestine might export five thousand cases of oranges by the next spring. Actually by 1937, the orange industry, due to Jewish enterprise, was exporting five million boxes. In 1944, Tel Aviv made Rabbi Wise an honorary citizen.

A young Jew volunteered to show the Wises the Vineyard of Abraham near Jerusalem. After seeing all the fascinating points of interest, Rabbi Wise apologized for detaining him from his midday meal. He laughed saying, "We have no noon lunch hour here." Rabbi Wise found that all he had eaten was coffee and bread for breakfast and tea and bread for dinner even though he had come from the United States where he had lived well. When Rabbi Wise asked, "Why endure starvation, seeing that plenty beckons from across the seas?" he replied, "Ah, but you forget that we are living in the land of our fathers!" This was an inspiring and thrilling answer to Rabbi Wise.

In the Church of the Holy Nativity, Dr. Wise saw Turkish troops on guard. He said: "These, we learned to our horror, were stationed there in order to prevent Greek and Roman Catholic, Armenian and Copt worshippers and even priests from slaying each other." Actually a year or two before, a bloody melee had started, because the priests of one communion had interfered with the lamps of another. Dr. Wise concluded: "How vain the hope of peace on earth as long as there is no actual peace among those who profess to be followers and priests of the Prince of Peace!"

The Palestine Rabbi Wise visited in 1913 was a land of "misery, disease, poverty, lawlessness, and ignorance." Upon returning to America, Dr. Wise redoubled his efforts for the Zionist movement. In 1922, the country became a mandated territory of Britain, and Rabbi Wise returned to visit it. He found that travel was easier, and disease and poverty had been greatly reduced due to the services of Jewish women through the Hadassah medical unit.

Rabbi Wise had found in 1913 that British officials showed their sympathy and helpfulness not to the homeless Jews who were seeking to rebuild their life in Palestine but to the Arab peasants living upon the lowest economic and educational level, who "had not been permitted to do anything for the land or for their own lives."

His third visit to Palestine was in 1935 and by that time he began to see the promise that the land held for the Jews. Hebrew University was functioning and growing. Jews who had been subjected to torture and humiliation in Nazi Germany were now building a new life amid ennobling and inspiring surroundings.

Dr. Wise was an ardent champion of freedom for Israel. He believed that as the years passed, the British Government was trying to whittle down the Balfour Declaration. In 1922, the Churchill White Paper cut off four-fifths of the territory in which the Jewish national home was to be established. When Ernest Bevin came to power, he showed what Wise called a "vicious anti-Zionism."

Over the years, Dr. Wise kept demanding that Britain fulfill its promises. Some of the British Zionists thought he was too critical, but Wise could not help feeling that "no nation is great enough to be free to do wrong."

Dr. Wise felt the tragedy of what he called, "the cruel British White Paper of 1939, which severely curtailed Jewish immigration to Palestine" and which, he said, was in effect a death sentence for scores if not hundreds of thousands of Jews who could have found life and safety in Palestine.

Dr. Wise invited the present writer to accompany him to Israel in 1946, and I accepted, but entrance was refused by the British and our visit never took place, much to my regret.

Nevertheless, in spite of all the obstacles, Israel became a reality, and few people are more responsible than Rabbi Wise himself. It has been a living demonstration of what a dedicated people can do to build justice, freedom, and happiness in a world fraught with conflict and hatred.

One of the things that always inspired me about Stephen Wise was his devoted work for labor in the United States. As far back as 1895 when some streetcar strikers were killed in Brooklyn, he spoke on the evil of shooting down strikers who were merely trying "to live decently and humanly." The result was that the treasurer of the Synagogue protested but Wise said, "I shall continue to speak for the workers whenever I come to feel that they have a real grievance and a just cause."

When the Los Angeles *Times Herald* building was dynamited in 1911, Rabbi Wise had this to say of the violence of the McNamaras: "As long as labor organizations are denied a hearing save just before elections; as long as they are treated with scorn and contumely; as long as they are cast out and denied, it is not to be wondered at that the leaders, finding themselves and their organizations outlawed, should in turn be guilty of outlawry."

He was determined that a Federal Commission on Industrial Relations be appointed. He finally succeeded, but he had to wait until Woodrow Wilson became President to secure what he considered a competent man appointed to the Commission.

In 1911, Stephen Wise was invited to speak before the New York Chamber of Commerce. In the audience were Andrew Carnegie, J. P. Morgan, and Charles Schwab among others. Stephen Wise spoke with great fearlessness that night and without mincing words.

> The conscience of the nation is not real unless the nation safeguards the workingman, safeguards him from peril of overwork, as well as from the occasional accidents of industry. The conscience of the nation is not vital unless we protect women and children in industry and protect them with half the thoroughness and generosity with which, for many decades, we have protected infant industries. We have not the right to speak of the importance of conserving the opportunity for initiative on the part of the individual as long as the masses of individuals are suffered to perish without the opportunity of real life. The aim of democracy is not to be the production of efficient, machine-like men in industry. The first business of democracy is to be the industry of turning out completely effective, because completely free, self-determining citizens.

When the Triangle fire occurred in a New York factory, many of the girls were burned to death because the doors had been locked so as to prevent goods from being removed by employees. Wise organized a permanent group and began the battle for safety legislation for factory workers.

In 1912, he was appointed as mediator in a lockout of some textile mills in Philadelphia. The weekly salaries at that time were: Winders and doublers, $4.75; reelers and lacers, $4.25; openers, shakers, and first-time spinners, $4.75; second-time spinners, $6.00; bobbin boys, $4.50; and learners $3.00 to start. He found that a large part of the employees were children and that their average wages were two and three dollars a week for forty-eight hours of work. All the recommendations of Rabbi Wise were ignored, and it was only after a strike that some concessions were granted.

In 1919, the steelworkers were still working a twelve-hour day. Rabbi Wise believed that they must be organized. A strike of steelworkers followed, but the steel companies used every method of violence against the workers. He decided to preach a sermon on the issue. He blasted the twelve-hour day and the seven-day week. He said the workers never had been free and were not free. "I charge the United States Steel Corporation with resorting to every manner of coercion and even to violence." As a result, Dr. Wise received letters of approval but many of "violent disapproval." A minister of religion in New York charged Dr. Wise with "prostituting the pulpit for personal notoriety." Resignations from the Synagogue poured in. One of the foremost Jewish financiers of the country resigned as did the Synagogue's first treasurer.

Shortly after his address, the Inter-Church World Movement investigated the facts in the steel strike and published a report. Stephen Wise felt that "from that moment on the Inter-Church World Movement was dead," because the conservative forces of the nation opposed taking action for truth and justice. His prediction proved accurate.

Rabbi Wise also took action in the Mooney case. He said: "I knew that gang of thieves and looters,—though they happened to be millionaires,—who were in control of the United Railways in San Francisco!" They were determined to destroy Mooney and had him sent to prison. Dr. Wise believed he was innocent and finally helped to secure his pardon. He quoted Senator Borah, Chairman of the Foreign Relations Committee of the United States Senate, as follows: "The charge of being a communist is coming to be the shield and protection for almost every kind of human exploitation. There would be no communism in this country that anyone need be disturbed about if conditions were what they ought to be and if justice was meted out as it ought to be."

It is small wonder that he was invited and spoke before the C.I.O. Convention in 1946. He also joined with those who founded the National Association for the Advancement of Colored People in 1909, because he was determined to fight against injustice to Negroes. Rabbi Wise said, "Discrimination of any kind is doubly damning,—it damns the man who discriminates, and it damns the man discriminated against."

I shall never forget that it was Rabbi Wise who founded the Jewish Institute of Religion in New York and was its honored president. He wanted the students to be trained in social service leadership and not under the influence of anti-Zionism. By the time World War II began, it had already graduated 150 students.

Rabbi Wise was also the inspiration and founder of the American Jewish Congress and its president. He later became president of the World Jewish Congress. By 1910 there were three million Jews in the United States. Many of them felt that there was no hope for the Jewish restoration of Palestine unless American Jews were organized and united. The preliminary conference was held in 1916, and Rabbi Wise gave the keynote address. On June 10, 1917, 350,000 Jews went to the polls in the United States to choose their representatives to the first American Jewish Congress which was held in 1918. The program adopted for submission to the Versailles Peace Conference included "the demand for full and equal civil, political, religious, and national rights for all citizens of any territory without distinction as to race or creed; and recognition of the historic claims of the Jewish people to Palestine." The Congress elected a distinguished delegation to the Peace Conference of which Rabbi Wise was one. After its inception the Congress stood guard over any developments affecting Jews anywhere in the world. It did everything in its power to help the Zionist movement in rebuilding Palestine. It attempted to rally all people, Jews and non-Jews alike, to an understanding of the menace of Hitler and fascism. It tried to make everyone aware that the security of no group could be assured unless the full rights of all were safeguarded.

In 1946, President Truman appointed Rabbi Wise to the Commission on Higher Education. He was instrumental in getting the Commission to recommend action against discrimination because of race, color or creed in its final report.

In the summer of 1942, Dr. Wise learned through Dr. Riegner, head of the Geneva offices of the World Jewish Congress, that the Nazis were planning to exterminate millions of Jews. In January, Riegner sent the American Jewish Congress a cable reporting that Jews were being killed at the rate of 6,000 a day. Later, it was learned that 70,000 Jews in France and Rumania could be rescued if funds were deposited in Switzerland to the credit of certain Nazi officials and not touched until the war was over. Rabbi Wise went to Washington and secured the approval of the President. In spite of this, due to blocking by State Department bureaucrats and the British Foreign Office it was not until five months later that they could go forward with the program. Dr. Wise concluded: "Let history, therefore, record for all time that were it not for State Department and Foreign Office bureaucratic bungling and callousness, thousands of lives might have been saved and the Jewish catastrophe partially averted."

Later Dr. Wise spoke out against the danger of an atomic war. He urged that Christianity be heard on this great issue. As he said: "The contest is far from being undefiled democracy versus pure dictatorship. The real dichotomy is between capitalist democracy and communist dictatorship—the question being whether capitalism can permanently endure as democratic and whether communism is bound to be permanently dictatorial. These are politico-economic problems that need not, cannot be resolved by war."

Only a very brief picture of his career has been given here. Are we day by day giving everything we have for liberty, justice, and human brotherhood as he did? Let us stop, look, and read more of his notable achievements[1] and then take action.

[1] Stephen S. Wise, *Challenging Years*. (New York, G. P. Putnam's Sons, 1949).

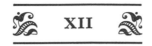

XII

NIKITA S. KHRUSHCHEV

ON JULY 24, 1957, an American delegation of professors, ministers, and others, which I was leading had a three-hour session with Mr. Khrushchev in the Kremlin. Here are some of the questions we asked Mr. Khrushchev and his answers.

Q. "What in your opinion are the principal obstacles to working out a program of disarmament and an end to the Cold War?"

A. "I don't know exactly what to advise on this question but the main thing is confidence in each other. The United States statesmen say that first you need proof, then confidence. But you can't have proof without confidence, and to try to secure it without confidence is self-defeating and going around in an endless circle. The main thing is that we must live on one and the same planet. The question is war or peace. If it is to be war, there can be no confidence. But we want peace, and peace means confidence and trust. When you come in here, we don't ask you to turn your pockets inside out because we don't trust you. We have confidence. Even in war when one side raises a white flag, there comes a time of confidence, and negotiations are carried on peacefully. Sometimes this backfires as it did for us in Budapest in World War II. Our Ambassador was killed, but this is a risk we have to take. We must still have hope. We must have trust before everything else, not controls but confidence. The more rigid control, the less confidence.

Q. "Would you be willing to end bomb tests permanently?"
A. "We would sign it tomorrow or better today without any conditions whatever."

Q. "What effective means of inspection and control do you propose?"
A. "We have proposed such a system. We have a vast territory and it is said in the United States, although I am not sure, that small tests go undetected, therefore there would need to be control posts on our territory to detect even the smallest tests. We have agreed to have U.S. inspectors on our territory at certain points so that even the smallest test would be detected but so far all our proposals put forth in London have received no answer."

Q. "Would the Soviet Union be willing to participate in a mammoth program for the development of the undeveloped areas of the world under the U.N.?"
A. "We have expressed readiness to do this if there is first disarmament, as this would release our funds to develop such countries and also would benefit the whole of humanity. A concrete proposal to this effect was put forth by Faure of France, and we supported it. The trouble is that as soon as we accept a proposal put forth by the West, the West denounces it. Many of our proposals were put forth earlier by the West and we were not willing to accept them then, but later when we proposed them, the West would not accept them."

Q. "What things do you think the U.S. could do more effectively to bring about peace?"

A. "The most important is to liquidate the vast trade barriers. Not because we need to sell to you or you need to buy from us. The quantity is not important, but trade brings confidence. In the old days traders were robbed and killed, but they still came and they brought confidence. To think that in this day and age we are not trading is fantastic. We are interested in your trade and you in ours. If you don't want strategic things to be sold this is all right, but a ban on trade can only exist if people are contemplating war. Even Soviet cooks are not allowed in the United States probably because the U.S. is afraid they will shake the foundations of its way of life! I met a farmer by the name of Garston who is a specialist on hybridization of corn. He was very nice and wanted to invite a group of agronomists to the U.S. They were refused entry by your government, and when he went to champion their entry, he had no luck. How can we improve prospects for peace when we can't even discuss corn."

Q. *"Under what conditions would you be willing to participate in an exchange of students and how many do you think you could take, perhaps 5,000?"*
A. "No, that would be too many as we would have to pay for their stay in the U.S. and that would be too expensive."

Q. *"But aren't you a rich country?"*
A. "Yes, but we have no dollars."

Q. *"Then couldn't we pay for your students and you pay for ours?"*
A. "All right, please. Some think we fear such exchanges and that our students will turn to capitalism. Perhaps some may, but this would be no tragedy and would not shake our country. Even if some decided to stay in your country,

and the same thing could happen with your students here, although I am sure you would pick the staunchest supporters of capitalism to send. This in no way stops our desire for these exchanges."

In our delegation we had one rather thin student, whose expenses had been paid by the Oberlin College student body of which he was a member. An amusing sidelight on Khrushchev's political skill was shown when the interview was over. As we all arose, he walked over to the student, threw his arms around him and hugged him, saying, "My dear young fellow! If you'll only stay in the Soviet Union, we'll fatten you up!"

In our appraisal of anyone, anywhere, our first question should be: What were the factors and characteristics of his background, social and personal? What conditioned his development? As far as one can determine, what are his objectives; is he sincere and honest? And to puncture our own self-righteousness in judging other human beings: "What would I have been like, what would I have accomplished, had I been born in his place and with his handicaps?"

Khrushchev was born on April 7, 1894, in the poverty-stricken village of Kalinova near Kursk, on the border of the Ukraine. His father was a coal miner, and Khrushchev did not even enter school until he was ten years of age and was working as a shepherd. Later on he became a pipefitter in a Donbas mine. He participated in strikes and studied in his free time. He was twenty-three when the Revolution started. In 1918, when he was twenty-four, he joined the Bolshevik party and fought in the civil war.

After the war ended he worked in an iron production plant, continuing his studies. He then went to the workers' school at the Donets Industrial Institute where he did so well that in 1929, at the age of thirty-five, he was sent to the Moscow Industrial Academy from which he graduated with distinction. He was invited to stay in Moscow and work for the party. Here he became acquainted with both Kaganovich and Malenkov. In 1934, he was elected the second ranking member of the Moscow Party Committee and a member of the Central Committee of the Communist Party of the Soviet Union. In 1935, he was elected First Secretary of the Moscow Party Committee. He had a good deal to do with the construction of the underground subway in Moscow which is one of the most beautiful in the world. For this, he was awarded the Order of Lenin.

In 1938, Khrushchev was elected as an "alternate" member of the Politburo; a year later he became a full member. He was now sent back to the Ukraine to head the party there. For three years he worked hard. During that time three thousand local party officials were dismissed on his charges of "having lost their vigilance." During this period, he was awarded the order of the Red Banner of Labor.

When Hitler struck, Khrushchev fought against the Germans in the Ukraine. He led the local partisan groups which kept attacking the German lines of communication. When Stalingrad was attacked, he served on the military council of the city and was later commissioned lieutenant general.

When the Germans were forced out of Russia, Khrushchev returned to the Ukraine to the work of restoring the country. Some 166,000 square miles of devastated cities, villages, farms, and wrecked communications had to be rebuilt. He was still chairman of the Council of Peoples' Commissars of the Ukraine. He also planned the liquidation of all Russians who had collaborated with the Nazis. In 1945, he was sent to Warsaw as head of a Russian delegation to discuss the restoration of that city. As a result of these discussions, Russia agreed to pay a major part of the reconstruction costs.

When he returned to the Ukraine, he was imbued with the idea of transforming all the farms into modernized villages where there would be electricity, hospitals, libraries, schools, and recreation facilities. It was a wonderful idea, but it interfered with the production of necessary food. The result was that Khrushchev was dismissed, and his place was taken by Kaganovitch in 1947.

Khrushchev continued to work for the party and in 1949, was back in Kiev, attending the Congress of the Ukrainian Communist Party. In December of that year he was appointed as Secretary of the Central Committee of the Communist Party in Moscow. It is not surprising that at the Nineteenth Congress of the Communist Party in Moscow in 1952, the three major speeches were made by Stalin, Malenkov, and Khrushchev. In view of the Stalin dictatorship at that time, it is interesting to note that Khrushchev had the courage to attack evils in the party. He vigorously condemned all officials who "thought themselves above the law." He assailed "nepotism and favoritism," saying: "It is a serious affair when friendship, family relationships and local ties are put before professional and political considerations."

Indirectly at that time, he even attacked Stalin, for he said: "There are quite a few leaders who think that the rules are not intended for them, assuming that everything is permitted to them. Such leaders turn the concerns of institutions entrusted to them into their own preserve, where they introduce their own regime, their own discipline to the background. They completely disregard both party decisions and the opinion of the party rank and file.

All sorts of scandalous irregularities happen where such bureaucrats with party cards in their pockets are in charge. The evil must be resolutely uprooted and causes great harm to the state and the party." He went on to say: "There are mistakes and shortcomings in the work of the party organization. The hushing up of these deficiencies is a disease which must be cured."

He pointed out another great evil in the communist system, the suppression of criticism from the rank and file. Said Khrushchev: "Too often criticism is stubbornly suppressed. There are more than a few who endlessly reiterate their loyalty to the party while hushing up criticism from below or preventing it altogether. There have been cases where honest people, good workers, have been removed only because they exposed shortcomings; when those who criticized individual workers have been victimized and have had to put up with intolerable conditions; when comrades who expressed correct and perfectly justified criticism have been compelled by threats to withdraw their criticism and made to promise that they would not repeat them." He also attacked graft and corruption by saying: "Some workers have been manipulating figures and giving misleading accounts of the fulfillment of economic plans." All this was said while Stalin was in power and was attending the Congress.

It is not surprising that after Stalin's death, Khrushchev reached the top and took Stalin's place nor that he later attacked Stalin for his dictatorship and "cult of personality."

In the 1956 Congress of the party, Khrushchev spoke for an entire day, both morning and afternoon.

He is discursive and eruptive in his remarks. Probably one reason he rose to the top is that after the death of Stalin, he was not afraid to take the reins, as many others were. Khrushchev tells an anecdote about four men who were in a prison cell and had dug a tunnel to escape. The person who went out first was likely to be shot, so none of the other three wanted to go. Khrushchev went.

He believes genuinely in peaceful coexistence and is unalterably opposed to nuclear war. This has subjected him to serious attacks from Red China and Albania. His great objective is to win over capitalism by economic competition. Khrushchev has repeatedly stated that he believes our grandchildren will all live under communism. This is the way he expresses it:

> The imperialists have now thought up the following theory. They say: "The Soviet Union now has the hydrogen bomb, so does the U.S.A., and so also now does Britain. Since the hydrogen bomb is a weapon of extraordinary power, neither side will use it, but they will scare each other with it, wage a cold war, and live on the principle of neither war nor peace." We Soviet people are against this principle. We are for peace and the banning of atomic and hydrogen weapons. We appeal to the U.S.A. and Britain to join us in this. We do not intend to blow up the capitalist world with bombs. If we catch up to the U.S. level of per capita output of meat, milk, and butter, we shall have shot a highly powerful torpedo at the underpinnings of capitalism.

Khrushchev has offered repeatedly to withdraw all troops from eastern Europe if the United States would withdraw its troops from western Europe, but this does not mean that he does not believe in the ultimate triumph of communism around the world.

Most people in the U.S. think of Khrushchev in terms of belligerence, intransigence, and adroit political maneuvers. His speech at the Twentieth Congress attacking Stalin is a good illustration of this. He described Stalin as a "criminal murderer," a supporter of "moral and physical annihilation." He said that under Stalin there were mass arrests and deportations of many thousands of people, executed without trial and without normal investigation, which created conditions of insecurity, fear, and even desperation.

It is commonly charged in the West that Khrushchev did nothing to prevent these injustices while Stalin was alive. As was noted before, his speech at the Congress in 1952 indirectly attacked, in party terms, leadership which assumed that everything is permitted to it. Khrushchev maintains that he did not know of many of the injustices while Stalin was alive. It must also be remembered that when he is your superior and can virtually say, "Off with his head," it is far more difficult to oppose a dictator.

Once in power, Khrushchev changed many conditions. All military tribunals were abolished. Commissions went into the prisons to check on whether the inmates had been unjustly imprisoned. All were given the right of retrial. The Ministry of the Interior lost a great deal of its power, and all its regional offices were made subject to the local Soviets.

Khrushchev decentralized the industrial organization of the state into 105 regional authorities. State-owned machine and tractor stations were generally abolished and given directly to the farmers. Electrification of the country and automation in the factories were started. All of these proposals were not made by dictatorial orders from above. To discuss the industrial changes, 614,000 meetings were called in the factories. Over 2 million people spoke on the proposals. Seventy thousand suggestions were made and considered, and in the end the opposition of the old leaders, Malenkov and Molotov, was swept aside.

Today, the Soviet trade unions are a real power. They have control over canteens, housing, restaurants, libraries, and stores. They negotiate collective bargaining agreements with management and see that they are carried out. No worker can be fired without their consent. They can always take action for the removal of any manager who "violates contracts, shows a bureaucratic spirit, or violates labor legislation."

Khrushchev is also strongly opposed to hooliganism on the part of the youth and to alcoholism. In a speech in 1958, he said: "Under the Soviet power, the material well-being and cultural level of the people have improved immeasurably. Hard drinking is now first of all a result of bad education. There are also cases of drunkenness and unworthy behavior among a part of our youth. There are young people who think that by using alcohol they display a kind of heroism; our youth despises such 'heroes.' Drinking is not a display of heroism, but a display of weakness and lack of will power."

Three months later, Khrushchev took stern measures against drunkenness. He said: "We will institute strict order in the streets. If a drunkard insults passers-by and acts like a hooligan, if this is his first offense, he will be taken to a special place where hooligans are set straight, sobered up, and fined according to the offense. If it is a case of more flagrant hooliganism, the agencies of public order will apply sterner measures. One cannot allow individuals to disgrace the Socialist State and our society by their unworthy acts. One must know how to behave."

All of this is not to gloss over his weaknesses. He is indiscreet, as he was when he pounded a table with his shoe at the United Nations. He sometimes has a quick temper. He is often untactful. When some Americans complained that too many Russian women worked, he replied, "Yes, our women work, and they are honest women—not like women in France, who are all whores!" In spite of his weaknesses, Khrushchev has common sense, a terrific drive, and unquenchable faith in a better future. He has tried to bring 87½ million acres of virgin land into agricultural production, and while the program has not been as successful as he had hoped for, it has not failed.

Nikita Khrushchev visited the United States in September, 1959, on the invitation of President Eisenhower. A dinner was given by the President for Khrushchev on the first evening of his visit, at which the Russian leader spoke quite frankly.

> We believe that our socialist system is better than yours. You think that your system is better than ours. What are we to do? Should we push the controversy over whose system is better to a fight between us on the battlefield? Would it not be better to let history settle the issue? I think that would be more reasonable. If you agree with that, we can build our relations on a basis of peace and friendship.

Most of the meetings at that time were very friendly, with one exception, the meeting with the trade union leaders. Khrushchev became angry at times, and he was not successful in winning the support of the trade unions. By way of contrast, the interview with Mr. Watson, president of International Business Machines, was most friendly. Mr. Watson said, "Just a month ago I visited Moscow again. There obviously has been a great deal of material progress in your country since the Second World

War. Anyone who visited the Soviet Union some time ago and revisits it now remarks on this fact. Americans consider this a happy event and not a challenge to our system."

Now, in appraising Khrushchev, we should recognize what he came out of. Had we been born in his place and subject to the same handicaps, would we have accomplished more? Mrs. Eleanor Roosevelt, for instance, thinks that had Khrushchev been born and reared in the United States, he would now be a great captain of industry. Whether this is true or not we do not know, but we should recognize that he is today one of the powerful rulers of a great nation, and every American ought to try and understand him, rather than hate him.

XIII

MILOVAN DJILAS

RECENTLY I HAD two long interviews with Milovan Djilas in Yugoslavia. He is one of the most colorful figures in the world today. Born in 1911, he grew up in a country of feuds and violence. His books *Land without Violence* and *The New Class* have been read throughout America. He himself wrote: "Life about us seethed with violence and cruelty. Death, including violent death, was a common though always disturbing event." He said: "I was born with blood on my eyes. My first sight was of blood. My first words were blood and bathed in blood." Actually his father's grandfather, his own two grandfathers, his father and his uncle were all killed.

His father's grandfather had been sent officially by the ruler of Montenegro to escort two Turks who had come on state business out of the country. Instead of living up to the trust that had been given him, he robbed and killed both of them. Then he in turn was killed under orders of the ruler of Montenegro for his betrayal of government orders. Djilas' grandfather Aleska then avenged this death by shooting the man who had killed his father. He in turn was later killed by being beaten on the head with a wooden mallet by Montenegrans who wanted revenge.

In the war of 1912, Djilas' father was assigned the task of inciting border clashes so that Montenegro would then have the excuse to declare war. Djilas has stated "Men became bad, rotten, unwilling to give one another air to breathe."

His father was seized by Austrian invaders in 1916 and was killed.

Small wonder that Djilas, the son, became a communist and took part in guerilla fighting with Marshal Tito. It is interesting that the Catholic archbishop, in trying to attack communism, actually influenced Djilas toward it. "Were not the first impulses toward Communism those arising out of a desire to put an end to the world of force and injustice and to realize a different world, one of justice, brotherhood, and love among men?" Milovan Djilas became a full-fledged communist at the beginning of his university studies. He wanted to change the barbarism of the society in which he lived, and he felt, "he could do so only in a movement that promised justice and had succeeded once through a great revolution. Communism was a new idea. It offered youth enthusiasm, a desire for endeavor and sacrifice to achieve the happiness of the human race." He helped to start the first communist youth movement in Yugoslavia even while the royal government was in power.

In 1933, he was arrested by the royal government, convicted and sentenced to three years at hard labor. After his release three years later, he continued his underground activity and was very successful in writing leaflets.

He met Joseph Broz, who was to become the famous Marshal Tito, but who at that time was secretary of the secret revolutionary Communist party.

When the Nazis occupied the country in 1941, Djilas participated in the partisan fight against them. He worked very closely with Tito in the staff headquarters. After the war, Tito made him Minister of Education and Propaganda. He became Vice-President and by 1953 was talked of as a possible successor to Tito. When Yugoslavia broke with the Soviet Union he wrote the articles defending this move. He maintained that it was Stalin who had betrayed Leninism and that the Yugoslavs had been true to communist principles.

Later on, Djilas began to be critical of the Yugoslav bureaucracy, charging that it was blocking true democracy. In January, 1954, he was stripped of all his government positions. He then took his party card and tore it to shreds before the communist officials. Later, because of an interview with a *New York Times* correspondent in which he urged the establishment of a rival, democratic, socialist party, he was arrested and sentenced for "hostile propaganda." However, he was released and it was only when he attacked the suppression of the Hungarian revolt in 1956 that he was again arrested. He had published an article in a New York magazine in which he wrote, "The revolution in Hungary means the beginning of the end of communism generally." This time he was sentenced for three years. While in prison, he smuggled out his book *The New Class* which maintained that communism was beginning to build a new class of exploiters who were misusing the people whom they had promised to liberate. For this offense, Djilas was sentenced to seven more years in prison.

When I saw him, he had been released on probation and given a very fine apartment in the capital city of Belgrade, where he lived with his wife. He had served four years in prison. He told me that he was treated very well while confined, although the food was not too good. When he suffered a sudden attack of appendicitis, he was sent to the finest doctor in Yugoslavia and to the best hospital for his operation. He seemed well and vigorous and was engaged in writing new books. Undoubtedly, he has to be careful in what he writes. He told me that he now feels he was too critical of the new regime in his book *The New Class.* In April, 1962, Djilas was again arrested for writing a book, *Conversations with Stalin,* which tells the story of his meetings with the dictator prior to the break with the Soviet Union in 1948.

I asked him to give me the heart of his approach to life, the essence of the philosophy that has motivated him, and the following is what he told me:

"I do not have a final, firm, and determined life goal. I hold that a fixed goal is superfluous even if it could be realized. By adhering to a goal too strictly, one must realize that it is only a step in the lifetime of the individual and humanity in general. Too firm adherence to a goal often leads to tyranny.

"The one thing that seems to me justified and reasonable in human existence is the adherence to the basic moral codes which have been developed by man together with the other equitable conditions of his existence in society. If this is a goal, I subscribe to it. However, this is not a goal to achieve but something to live by, because these moral codes are prerequisites for inner peace and the real happiness of man—all those who decided to give them up destroyed the basic premises of their own existence.

"On account of all this, the most difficult obstacles I have had, I discovered within myself. Many of these I have overcome, many times I have been in error, but often I have been on the right road. It seems that such is the fate of man and humanity in ever-present clashes between good and truth versus the material conditions of life. I have seen and lived through much, probably more evil than good; this did not destroy but strengthened my belief in the power of man's inevitable struggle against evil—

yesterday, today, and tomorrow—from the beginning to the end of mankind.

"Man, in spite of all outside influences, can find an irresistible strength within himself. In the world and in society, man is a world within himself.

"The clash with my own political comrades which came about in January, 1954, was the hardest to bear in my life, because with them I had shared the evil as well as the good. This was a struggle for adherence to ideals which I consider the most far-reaching and important in my life. This was a trial not only of my conscience but the strength of my convictions, qualities, and capabilities. I could not say that this trial could have been resolved any better. I tried everything I could but found that this was something that went beyond my own self. It was hard but inevitable. In my own country, I became a stranger and in my circle, an outcast. I never regretted this, because from it I retained my own true self, though wounded spiritually and trampled down.

"I was helped the most by those who were outside the immediate struggle; these were the small, unknown people who in passing gave me their support, encouragement, and reassurance. Living in the midst of a dedicated closed society and as a result of my clash with this society, I was left without friends or even acquaintances. However, I did find support only in those who did not have power or influence, yet these people were powerful and rich in the sense that they were morally above all other human beings. Had I done otherwise, I could not have gone on being as I am in the world I existed in.

"Because men are living in conditions which change from day to day, these are times of struggle which can involve us all and be seen in every nook and cranny of this globe. It seems that these struggles are one way of unifying mankind. The fight will inevitably attain cosmic proportions, for strong and restless is man. Without believing in a utopian ideal society or eternal peace, I am completely sure that in the world of tomorrow the struggle for survival will be easier and more successful, which gives hope that the people will be able and can adhere more consistently to moral and spiritual values.

"For that future world, for the peace of tomorrow, it will be possible to do much, and it is in the process of being done. Broadening divergent existing and opposing systems would be the most fruitful and important task, though we are still far from doing this. Men with knowledge and ability to write will have to want to accept this, which would be a great accomplishment in itself. If social systems as yet cannot be mixed or integrated, then it is important for the people who are most wise to passionately and objectively support that which is the common good of all peoples and nations regardless of how or where they live.

"Many things have changed my life, but in spite of this and from my own viewpoint, something always remained the same—something did not change. Within me there was always some kind of opposition or incapability to adjust to conditions of injustice.

"Of course if I could live my life over again, there are many things that I would do differently. This in itself is a wish. Probably I wouldn't be able to change anything if I were as I am and conditions were the same. I lived my life as well as I could. It wasn't bad, even not hard, though it could have been more consistent.

"It is important that we do what we can to be consistent with our conscience. We must broaden the boundaries of human freedom and stir the human conscience for justice everywhere."

So much for Djilas' philosophy. He believes that, instead of fighting world wars and trying to annihilate rival economic systems, we should learn to live with them and they will gradually change. He has spent years in prison, but we can all agree that he has had the courage and fortitude to speak the truth as he saw it.

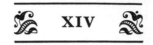

XIV

MAHATMA GANDHI

A RESOLUTION FOR EVERY DAY

Let then our first act every morning be to make the
following resolve for the day:

> *I shall not fear anyone on earth.*
> *I shall fear only God.*
> *I shall not bear ill will towards anyone.*
> *I shall not submit to injustice from anyone.*
> *I shall conquer untruth by truth.*
> *And in resisting untruth I shall put up with*
> *all suffering.*

> *For a bowl of water give a goodly meal;*
> *For a kindly greeting bow thou down with zeal;*
> *For a simple penny pay thou back with gold;*
> *If thy life be rescued, life do not withhold.*
> *Thus the words and actions of the wise regard,*
> *Every little service tenfold they reward.*
> *But the truly noble know all men as one,*
> *And return with gladness good for evil done.*
> (Anon.)

MAHATMA GANDHI believed in *satyagraha* or "truth power"
or "soul force". He wrote that it ". . . is the vindication
of truth not by infliction of suffering on the opponent but
on one's self." The enemy must be "weaned from error by

patience and sympathy." Gandhi always believed that the means and ends must be consistent. This ruled out war. He believed that the morals and practices of the individual, group, and nation must be the same.

How did I come to see Gandhi? It was because I adopted a principle in my first college year at Oberlin. I would try to help everyone I met. This included using every opportunity that came my way, whether or not I knew the person. I made up my mind that I would never eat alone anywhere in the world. This meant that if I were in a restaurant, I would look over everyone seated there and then pick out someone who was eating alone and ask if I might join him. I was almost never refused. Once seated, I would try to get acquainted and help the other person. As often as not this would culminate in his helping me. It also took me to India to see Gandhi.

During the Second World War, I was sent by the American Y.M.C.A. to Russia on a special mission. In order to be able to go I had to represent a newspaper, so I secured credentials from the Toronto *Star*. Enroute, I had to stop in London. It was on a Sunday, and I entered a restaurant for lunch. I looked over all of the tables and spotted a lone Indian seated by himself. He very graciously invited me to sit with him. Since India was at that time under the complete domination of England, I spoke of how wonderful it would be if India could some time be free and independent. The Indian warmed up quickly, and we became great friends. I found out that he was working in the British Foreign Office, and he asked if I would like to meet Lord Wavell, who had just been appointed viceroy for all India. Since I was representing a newspaper, I said I would be delighted. He replied, "Be at my office at three o'clock."

At three o'clock, I met Lord Wavell, Lady Wavell, and

their daughter. I asked Lord Wavell if I could have an interview with him for the Canadian press. He replied, "Not now, since I have just been appointed, and it might cost me my assignment. But come to India, and I'll be glad to give you an interview." I asked Lord Wavell, "Do you really mean this invitation?" "Mean it?" he said. "Of course, I mean it!" "Well then," I answered, "would you mind calling in your secretary and writing a formal invitation to me?" He responded immediately, and I left with an official invitation from the British government to visit India. A year and a half later I was on my way to India in a British plane, and my fare was even paid by the British government.

On the plane was an American officer, and he invited me to stay with him overnight at the U.S. Army base in India. I accepted his offer gladly, since I had traveled all over the world and had learned to be very careful in eating, especially in Asia and the poverty-stricken countries. I felt a meal in a United States Army base would be far safer. That night we had a fabulous dinner in the officer's mess. Besides delicious steak, they served a beautiful green salad, but I had noticed that there were many flies and that the waiters were all Indians. I did not eat the salad. The U.S. officer who had traveled with me on the plane asked, "Why don't you eat your salad?" I responded that in the course of traveling all over the world I had learned to be careful about eating things that were not cooked. He immediately called me "a fool" and said I did not "appreciate that this was a U.S. military base." Nevertheless, I stuck to my resolution; the end result was that I was not sick a day, but the very next day my officer friend was taken to the hospital with amoebic dysentery.

Lord Wavell was most kind to me while I was in India.

He permitted me to go anywhere and even to visit the prisons and talk with political prisoners. The one person whom I was not permitted to visit, because they said he was too "dangerous" was the present prime minister of India, Jawaharlal Nehru.

It was not long before I was visiting Gandhi, who impressed me as one of the most sincere men I had ever met. He said that the three most powerful influences in his life were the Bible, Ruskin, and Tolstoy. He added: "The Sermon on the Mount went straight to my heart. The verses, 'But I say unto you, that ye resist not evil. But whosoever shall smite thee on thy right cheek, turn to him the other also. And if any man . . . take away thy coat, let him have thy cloak also,' delighted me beyond measure. That renunciation was the highest form of religion appealed to me greatly."

Gandhi was born in 1869. At the age of thirteen, he was married by his parents. Just before his nineteenth birthday, he sailed for England to study law, having taken an oath that he would not touch "wine, women, or meat." Gandhi observed his oath faithfully. In 1891, he was admitted to the British bar and without waiting a day, he sailed for India.

He tried to practice law but without too much success. When one firm offered to send him to South Africa as its lawyer, he accepted gladly. He met with experiences there that transformed his career. He said: "I recall particularly one experience that changed the course of my life. That experience fell to my lot seven days after I arrived in South Africa. On the train, I had a first-class ticket but not a bed ticket. At Maritzburg, where the beddings were issued, the guard came and turned me out and asked me to go to the van compartment. I would not go, and the train steamed away leaving me in the shivering cold. Now, the creative experience comes there. I was afraid for my very life. I entered the dark waiting room. There was a white man in the room. I was afraid of him. 'What is my duty?' I asked myself. Should I go back to India or should I go forward with God as my helper and face whatever is in store for me? I decided to stay and suffer. My active nonviolence began from that date. And God put me through the test during that journey. I was severely assaulted by the coach attendant for my moving from the seat he had given me. That was one of the richest experiences of my life." (*Harijan,* December 10, 1938).

Gandhi remained in South Africa for twenty-one years, working for the Indian community. The first public speech he made, within one week following his arrival, was addressed to Indians on white discrimination. In the Natal province, an Indian had to carry a pass if he appeared on the streets after 9:00 P.M. When Gandhi went to Lionel Curtis, head of the Transvaal Asiatic Department, to try to convince him of the admirable character of the Indians, Curtis replied, "Mr. Gandhi, you are preaching to the converted. It is not the vices of the Indians that Europeans in this country fear, but their virtues." Apparently the white population was afraid that the Indians might furnish leadership in the struggles of the Negroes to gain equal rights in South Africa.

It must not be thought that what was happening in South Africa is peculiar to that country. When I went to Florida in 1962, I found that in many communities, a Negro was not allowed to walk on the street in the evening unless he carried a pass. He could not drink water from the public fountain or use any of the public toilets. It is so easy for the citizens of the United States to cast aspersions on the evils in other countries and forget their own.

Gandhi reminded me of this when I discussed the terrible conditions of the outcasts. He spoke of the blacks who had been torn from their homes in South Africa, sold to traders for a dollar apiece, and then sold in United States ports for $200 each. Sometimes half the cargo would die enroute, but even so enormous profits were made. The Negroes were considered "black cattle," so it did not make any difference. Gandhi implied that if he were in the United States, he would take action against our color discrimination.

When Gandhi returned to India to bring back his two sons, he told the Indian people of the terrible plight of their fellow countrymen in Africa. His speeches were reported back in Africa, and when he returned from India and his boat docked, the whites demanded that he be denied entry and his steamer be sent back. After some time, Gandhi was allowed to disembark, and he was then attacked by a mob. He was beaten and kicked into unconsciousness. He was taken to the home of an Indian, where a mob surrounded the house, yelling, "We'll burn him!" Later on others began to sing, "We'll hang old Gandhi on the sour apple tree." Fortunately, two constables were able to take him out through the back door and succeeded in getting him to the police station, where he stayed for three days.

Actually, Gandhi was doing remarkably well financially in his legal work in South Africa. He was making twenty-five to thirty thousand dollars a year. About this time he read John Ruskin's book, *Unto This Last*. It made a powerful impression on him, and he decided to buy a farm and live simply. In 1906, at the age of thirty-seven, Gandhi decided to abstain from all further sexual intercourse and remained true to his vow.

Leo Tolstoy also influenced Gandhi, especially through his book, *The Kingdom of God Is Within You.* Tolstoy maintained that a real Christian is one who "enters into no dispute with his neighbor, he neither attacks nor uses violence; on the contrary, he suffers himself without resistance and by his very attitude toward evil, not only sets himself free but helps to free the world at large from all outward authority."

Gandhi struggled for freedom for the Indians in South Africa, and finally, with the aid of General Smuts, secured the passage of a law in 1914 giving Indians more rights than they ever had before. Smuts paid a great tribute to Gandhi when he wrote of him: "He never forgot the human background of the situation, never lost his temper or succumbed to hate, and preserved his gentle humor in the most trying situations. His manner and spirit even then as well as later, contrasted markedly with the ruthlessness and brutal forcefulness which is in vogue in our day."

Gandhi returned to India in 1915 and began his campaign for a free India. Some eighty-five percent of the people in India were diseased, illiterate, poverty-stricken, and dying early in life. Gandhi wanted to help them, and he gave up all of his property and went to live in an ashram in the country. Over a million peasants rented land from British owners. Fifteen percent of their land had to be sown with indigo and the harvest of this crop given to the British owners. But when synthetic indigo was developed, the British ordered the peasants to cease production of indigo. At the same time, the landlords raised their rents. The peasants protested. They were then beaten, their houses looted, and their cattle seized. Gandhi went to Champaran in 1917 to help the peasants. He stayed there seven months until he got the landlords to refund twenty-five percent of the rent increases already made and to agree not to make any further ones.

After World War I was over, Indians expected more civil liberty from the British. Instead, the wartime restrictions were continued. Gandhi proposed a temporary strike with factories to be idle, ships to stand unloaded, and all economic activity to be suspended. This would be a mass demonstration lasting from one to three days.

The British General Dyer decided to use military force against one such crowd in the Punjab. His soldiers fired 1,650 rounds into the crowd, killing 379 persons and wounding 1,137. Gandhi answered this with a program of complete boycott of everything British. He urged: "Refuse to take British goods or accept British jobs, boycott British schools and courts." The result was that hundreds of Indians, including Nehru, left the British courts; Indian youth left their classrooms. Indians went into the villages urging noncooperation. This included nonpayment of taxes and nonpurchase of British goods.

For seven months Gandhi traveled, speaking to hundreds of thousands of Indians and urging this program. During all of this time, his three meals each day were exactly the same, consisting of three slices of toast, two oranges, some grapes or raisins, and sixteen ounces of goat's milk. In 1922, Gandhi was arrested by the British, tried, and sentenced to six years in prison. Here, in part, is his statement during the trial.

> I came reluctantly to the conclusion that the British connection has made India more helpless than ever before, politically and economically. . . . She has become so she has little power of resisting famines. Before the British advent, India spun and wove in her millions of cottages just the supplement she needed for adding to

her meagre agricultural resources. . . . Many British officials in India do not know that a subtle but effective system of terrorism and an organized display of force on the one hand, and the deprivation of powers of retaliation and self-defense on the other, have emasculated the people and induced in them the habit of simulation.

Gandhi went on to say that he considered it "an honor to be disaffected" and requested "the severest penalty."

After he had been confined for twenty-two months in prison, he had an appendicitis attack and the British decided to release him.

Gandhi then began his campaign to better the conditions of the poor. He promoted the spinning wheel which he felt would give work to the millions who were idle at least four months in the year. Gandhi opposed communism, because it did not give enough freedom to the individual. He said: "Bolshevism is the necessary result of modern materialistic civilization. Its insensate worship of matter has given rise to a school which has been brought up to look upon materialistic advancement as the goal of life . . . I prophesy that if we disobey the law of the final supremacy of spirit over matter, of liberty and love over brute force, in a few years' time we shall have Bolshevism rampant in this land which was once so holy."

In 1930, Gandhi decided to embark upon a campaign of civil disobedience. But before doing so he wrote a letter to the British viceroy explaining his reasons: "Before embarking upon civil disobedience, I would fain approach you and find a way out. I cannot intentionally hurt anything that lives, much less human beings, even though they may do the greatest wrong to me and mine. Whilst, therefore, I regard the British rule as a curse, I do not intend to harm a single Englishman or any legitimate interest he may have in India. And why do I regard the British rule as a curse? It has impoverished the dumb millions by a system of progressive exploitation and by a ruinous expensive military and civil administration which the country can never afford. It has reduced us politically to serfdom. It has sapped the foundations of our culture . . ."

When I saw Gandhi in his ashram in 1944, he told me, "All India is a prison house, and the British are the jail keepers, but we will secure our freedom by nonviolent means." Actually, Mahatma Gandhi had inspired millions to united effort and sacrifice for freedom. The British had even made it a crime to use salt not purchased from the government salt monopoly. Gandhi had openly made salt from the ocean and violated the regulation, for which he had again been jailed.

While I was at his ashram Gandhi held a prayer meeting each day in which all faiths participated. He even had communists attend his ashram. Gandhi said, "I am a Christian, a Hindu, a Moslem, and a Jew." "Jesus," he said, "possessed a great force, the love force, but Christianity became disfigured when it went to the West; it became the religion of kings."

Gandhi was one of the most dedicated men I have ever met. He was utterly honest and sincere. He wanted to help the masses of the people regardless of what it cost him. I agree with Nehru's statement about him: "Through nation-wide action he sought to mold the millions and largely succeeded in doing so and changing them from a demoralized, timid and hopeless mass, bullied and crushed by every dominant interest, and incapable of resistance, into a people with self-respect and self-reliance, resisting tyranny and capable of united action and sacrifice for a larger cause." Nehru says that thanks to Gandhi there was relatively little of violence and hatred in winning freedom in India. In a letter written in 1936, Nehru stated: "The British government has functioned in a purely fascist way during the past six years." In spite of this, Gandhi was determined to win India's freedom by nonviolence and good will.

After World War II, India achieved its independence on August 15, 1947, but unfortunately Pakistan became an independent state instead of remaining part of the Indian nation. Gandhi drew up an eight-point program on which Hindus and Moslems must come to agreement. Most of the points favored the Moslems. They were to be given complete freedom, and the 550 million rupees due to Pakistan were to be paid. This so enraged Hindu partisans that a Gandhi meeting was bombed, and later Gandhi was shot fatally by Goodse, the editor of a Hindu weekly in Poona.

Gandhi is dead, yet his spirit still lives and reverberates around the world. Gandhi attempted to win independence for India and the struggle for India's internal unity. He won the first, and the battle for the second is still going on. The tactics he used were: self-sacrifice, or literally following the way of the Cross; simplicity; and always following the path of truth and soul force. Gandhi believed in sharing the lot of the poor. He also believed in responding to the sins of others, not by name-calling and militant aggression, but by taking on self-suffering to change them.

In this age of atomic and bacteriological warfare, humanity faces the alternative of either taking the way of Jesus and of Gandhi or of being annihilated. Thus far the nations of the world, including the United States, are taking the way of military force and psychological violence compounded by hatred and cold war. Each year we spend more and more on weapons for military power. All history proves that if both sides continue to arm to the teeth, world war results. If this eventuates in our age, we will destroy all that is best that man has produced through the centuries.

Nehru was right when he said that Gandhi combined the Sermon on the Mount with effective action. He used these methods: the refusal to subordinate means to an end; the constant endeavor to lessen ill will and fear; the continuous willingness to make friends of his opponents; and yet at the same time take effective and dynamic action. One of Gandhi's most famous sayings is: "Hatred ever kills, love never dies. Such is the vast difference between the two. What is obtained by love is retained for all time. What is obtained by hatred proves a burden in reality, for it increases hatred. The duty of a human being is to diminish hatred and to promote love."

Will the world return good for evil? Will we try to win the communists by being friends with them and showing them our love? Placing Red China behind a stone wall of excommunication, not allowing Americans to visit her country, not permitting China to join the United Nations, are neither the way of Jesus nor that of Gandhi. It is the way of hatred and if we persist, it will lead ultimately to annihilation.

Gandhi once wrote E. Stanley Jones: "Saul became Paul, not by an intellectual effort but by something touching his heart. All I can say is that my heart is absolutely open; I have no axes to grind; I want to find truth, to see God face to face."

Gandhi's life is his message to mankind. When you, who are reading these words, finish your earthly career, what will your life message have carried to all those whose lives you have touched?

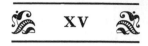

XV

MARTIN LUTHER KING

THE UNITED STATES is a nation with a background of slavery, and the consequences of this terrible evil still remain to haunt and plague the southern states. Martin Luther King's great grandfather and great grandmother were both slaves, but after the Civil War ended, Rev. King's ancestors advanced, and his father became pastor of a Baptist church of 5,000 members in Atlanta, Georgia.

Martin Luther King is the youngest of all the leaders included in this book. He was born in Atlanta, Georgia, on January 15, 1929. His father was actively opposed to the discrimination that existed there against Negroes. Martin was influenced by the examples of both his father and his mother. She also had grown up in a minister's home.

For six years, Martin attended the public schools for Negroes in Atlanta. They were badly overcrowded, and the teaching was poor. He was then sent to a private school. As a matter of fact, at that time there was only one Negro high school in all Atlanta, and that had 6,000 students. Martin worked outside of school. He had a paper route. During the summers, he worked eight hours a day for pay. For this, he received only sixty cents an hour, although all white workers were being paid from eighty cents to one dollar and twenty cents per hour. The year before he went to Morehouse College, he worked in the tobacco fields of Simsbury, Connecticut, and saved four hundred dollars. His parents gave him the rest of the money he needed. While in college he maintained a "B" average and was in the glee club, the Y.M.C.A., and the N.A.A.C.P. During his freshman year, he thought of going into medicine or law as a career. He wondered whether religion could be intellectually respectable. He revolted against the backwardness and emotionalism of the Negro churches. Nevertheless, by the end of his junior year, he had decided to enter the ministry and was ordained during his senior year.

He was profoundly influenced by President Benjamin Mays of Morehouse College and by Dr. George Kelsey, one of his professors who taught him that religion could be both emotionally satisfying as well as intellectually sound. He graduated from Morehouse in 1948 and then went to Crozier Theological Seminary, where he graduated at the top of his class. For his achievement, he received an honorary award and a cash prize. He also received the J. Lewis Crozier Fellowship and then went on to Boston University to study for his Ph.D., which he completed in 1954. His dissertation was written on the subject of "The Compassion of God."

Dr. King told me that ninety-five percent of the Negro ministers have not had theological education and ninety percent have not even been to college. Thus, many of these ministers may have no interest in the "Social Gospel." Martin was influenced by his father, who led the struggle for the equalization of Negro and white teachers' salaries. He was also influenced profoundly by the writings of Walter Rauschenbush.

After completing studies for his doctorate, he received offers from three colleges: one, a teaching post; one, a deanship; and the other, an administrative position. He turned down all of these to accept a post in the Dexter Avenue Baptist Church in Montgomery, Alabama. Previously, he had done all of the preaching in his father's church in Atlanta for three successive summers.

It is important to understand how Martin Luther King became so identified with the integration movement. As a very small child, prior to going to school, Martin had had as inseparable playmates two white boys whose parents had a store across the street from his home. Suddenly, the white parents put a stop to his playing with their children. He could not understand this and finally asked his mother, who told him about segregation. He learned about the divided schools, the movies, the restaurants, and the housing, and that segregation was the rule of life in this southern area. However, his mother assured him, "You are as good as anyone."

Martin remembered how when he was very young his father took him to a shoestore, and they sat down in chairs at the front. The clerk finally told them he could not serve them unless they moved to the rear. This, the father refused to do, and the clerk refused to sell them any shoes.

Even before Martin was born, his father had refused to ride on the city busses after seeing how some of the Negro passengers were attacked. He had been a leader in the struggle to equalize teachers' salaries and had helped to eliminate discrimination in the elevators in the court house.

Martin hated the discrimination in the South and was sorely tempted to accept a pastorate in Detroit. However, as we have noted, he finally decided to serve in Montgomery.

He married Coretta Scott. Her father had run a trucking concern, a grocery store, and a chicken farm in Marion,

Alabama. She went to Antioch College, and then to the New England Conservatory of Music and it was there that Martin fell in love with her.

For some months after he took the pastorate, he also worked on his Ph.D. dissertation. To show his drive and energy, consider the program he followed: He arose at five-thirty every morning, working for the first three hours of the day on his dissertation; then, again in the evening he would spend another three hours on it. The rest of the time during the day was spent in regular church work which included visiting, marriages, funerals, weekly services, as well as all the other details of serving a big church. On Wednesday, Thursday, and Friday, he also had to spend time on the preparation of his Sunday sermon, which he would finish writing Saturday evening.

Montgomery had both the Maxwell and the Gunter Air Force Bases in the vicinity, and these exercised a powerful effect on the city. The Montgomery Chamber of Commerce found that these two bases were responsible for providing fifty-eight million dollars worth of business during the single year of 1955. One out of every fourteen civilians in Montgomery worked at one or the other of these bases.

Montgomery has a large cattle market which handles thirty million cattle annually. The Negroes, of course, have inferior positions. Sixty-three percent of the Negro women workers are domestics and forty-eight percent of the Negro men are laborers or domestic workers. The middle income for the whites in 1950 was $1,730, while for the Negroes it was $970. Ninety-four percent of the whites have flush toilets in their homes, but only thirty-one percent of the Negroes have such accommodations.

The Negro and white communities were completely

segregated. The schools, the busses, the taxis, and all the organizations and even the churches were segregated. By 1940 there were only 2,000 Negro voters in all Alabama, and while this number had increased to about 50,000 by 1958, it was only a small fraction of the Negro population. In Montgomery County only 2,000 out of 30,000 Negroes were registered, and all sorts of blocks were put in their way.

In order to deal with these problems Martin Luther King set up a social and political action committee in his church. This committee kept the importance of being registered voters before the membership. It also arranged for forums and mass meetings to discuss social problems. Before the year was over, the committee was also publishing a bi-weekly newsletter in which major political and social issues were discussed and which went to every member of the church.

King also took a prominent part in the National Association for the Advancement of Colored People in the United States and was elected to its executive committee. This group defended Jeremiah Reeves, a Negro boy of sixteen, who had been arrested and charged with raping a white woman. The N.A.A.C.P. believed him to be innocent, but he was finally executed. By contrast, white men accused of raping Negro girls were seldom even arrested and, if arrested, were released without ever being brought to trial.

King also belonged to the Council on Human Relations which sought to change the attitudes of the white population through education.

An influential white citizen protested to King: "Over the years we have had such peaceful and harmonious race relations here. Why have you and your associates come in to destroy this long tradition?"

King answered: "You have never had real peace in Montgomery. You have had a sort of negative peace, in which the Negro too often accepted his state of subordination. But this is not true peace. True peace is not merely the absence of tension; it is the presence of justice. The tension we see in Montgomery today is the necessary tension that comes when the oppressed rise up and start to move forward toward a permanent, positive peace."

King believed that this was what Jesus meant when he said, "I have not come to bring peace but a sword." In other words, Jesus didn't mean that he brought a physical sword but as King says, "A conflict is precipitated between the old and the new. Whenever I come, a division sets in between justice and injustice. I have come to bring a positive peace which is the presence of justice, love, yea, and even the Kingdom of God."

Not long after King's arrival in Montgomery, a high school girl, Claudette Colvin, was arrested because she had refused to relinquish her seat on a bus to a white passenger. The girl was sent to jail.

This resulted in the formation of a citizens' committee on which Dr. King served, to talk with the bus company. They succeeded in getting the girl released with a suspended sentence, but the policy of segregation remained unchanged.

On December 1, 1955, another Negro who was sitting in the first seat assigned to Negroes was asked to move to the rear of the bus, because there were whites standing. Mrs. Rosa Parks, the passenger involved, refused to do so and was arrested. This sparked a boycott of all busses on the part of the Negroes of Montgomery. A meeting was held in Rev. King's church, with most of the Negro ministers attending, at which it was decided to arrange to have the Negro taxis transport people who previously had ridden on the busses. King had seven thousand leaflets mimeographed in his church urging people not to use the busses. A mass meeting was called, and all the Negroes heard about it since it was given publicity in the press.

At this meeting, the Montgomery Improvement Association was organized. Dr. King gave the main address and in closing said, "If you will protest courageously, and yet with dignity and Christian love, when the history books are written in future generations, the historians will have to pause and say, 'There lived a great people—a black people, —who injected new meaning and dignity into the veins of civilization.' This is our challenge and our overwhelming responsibility."

The resolution to boycott the busses was carried unanimously, and when the question was finally carried to the United States Supreme Court, this tribunal ruled that discrimination on busses was unconstitutional.

Dr. King believes that his successful struggle against discrimination on the Montgomery busses is perhaps the greatest achievement of his life, because it may prove to be the psychological turning point in the campaign of the Negro people for equal justice. It has given Negroes all over the United States a new sense of dignity and the feeling that it is possible for them to unite for positive achievements.

He feels that he will see the end of all segregation in his lifetime and within ten years integration in all urban areas. He is convinced that before long there may be five to ten Negro Congressmen from the South. If literacy tests, which today may be used to bar Negroes from voting whether they can read and write or not, are ended and the Justice Department vigorously enforces voting rights, the

Negro will become such an important power in politics that the white politicians may be willing to compromise and agree to the election of some Negroes. He believes that if we can get genuine racial equality in all of our states, then we could do far more to build international peace. He says, "As long as racial injustice persists, we can never have world peace. The situation in South Africa today is one of the worst in the whole world."

Dr. King was elected president of the Montgomery Improvement Association and applied the Gandhian philosophy of nonviolence to his methods of struggle.

In his early teens in Atlanta, he had seen Negroes brutally lynched. He had seen the operation of the Ku Klux Klan and the brutality of the police towards Negroes. This had brought him perilously close to hating the whites. But then he realized that the poor whites were also being exploited economically. In the theological seminary, he began to read Karl Marx and became convinced "that truth is found neither in Marxism nor in traditional capitalism. Each represents a partial truth. Historically, capitalism failed to see the truth in collective enterprise, and Marxism failed to see the truth in individual enterprise."

When King heard Mordecai Johnson, president of Howard University, speak on the life and teachings of Mahatma Gandhi, he went out and bought all the books he could on Gandhi. He was fascinated by Gandhi's method of nonviolent resistance. Previously King had thought that nonviolent resistance would work only between individuals; now he became convinced that it was a powerful and effective force on a group scale. When King read Reinhold Niebuhr, he was certain that Niebuhr was wrong. Niebuhr interpreted pacifism as a sort of "naïve trust in the power of love." King felt pacifism was not nonresistance to evil but nonviolent resistance to evil.

The points that Dr. King makes when he analyzes nonviolence are as follows:

1. Nonviolent resistance does not mean submission; it means *resistance*.

2. It does not seek to humiliate an opponent but to win his friendship and understanding.

3. It concentrates on the forces of evil rather than on those who are doing the evil.

4. It accepts suffering without retaliation.

5. It avoids not only physical violence but internal violence of spirit. It uses *agape*—love for all men. *Agape*, King believes, is the only cement that can hold a broken community together.

6. It maintains that the universe is on the side of justice and true brotherhood transcends race and color.

In an attempt to break the boycott of the busses, the authorities arrested Dr. King on a false charge of speeding. His house was bombed but fortunately no one was killed. Later, mass violence was used by the city government to break the movement. There was the case of a man who boarded the bus, whereupon the driver ordered him to get off and enter the bus through the rear door. The Negro refused and asked that his dime be returned to him for he said he wanted to walk. The police were called, and the man was shot and later died from his wounds. Dr. King himself was arrested eight times. In Montgomery, policemen twisted his arm and kicked him into his cell. When he was taken to the state penitentiary, he was both handcuffed and chained.

On June 4, 1956, by a two-to-one decision, a Federal court decided that bus segregation in Montgomery was unconstitutional. This was later affirmed by the United States Supreme Court. This decision reached Montgomery on December 20th, and King describes what happened:

> By December 28th the first few days of peaceful compliance had given way to a reign of terror. City busses were fired on throughout the city, especially in poorly lighted sections. A teenage girl was beaten by four or five white men as she alighted from a bus. A pregnant Negro woman was shot in the leg.

On January 9th, while King was in Atlanta, he was informed that both the home and the church of Rev. Ralph Abernathy in Montgomery had been bombed. Later, three other Negro Baptist churches were bombed.

The city fathers used this as an excuse to order all busses off the streets. Finally, when bombings began again, the city authorities made some arrests of white men. In spite of the fact that the men signed confessions, the jury returned verdicts of "not guilty."

Gradually the bombings ceased and the busses began operating normally. The struggle for justice had been won by the Negroes.

Of course, there are many other things that still remain to be done. The Montgomery Improvement Association headed by Dr. King has tackled the issue of the right of Negroes to vote. But of the two thousand they have sent to register, only ten percent have succeeded in getting their names on the list of eligible voters.

Another issue is that of complete school integration. King has said: "If every church and synagogue had developed an action program; if every civic and social welfare organization, every labor union and educational institution, had worked out concrete plans for implementing their righteous resolutions then Federal troops would not have had to be sent to Central High School." (Little Rock, Arkansas.)

Dr. King indicates that the areas of greatest resistance to racial justice are Georgia, Alabama, Mississippi, Louisiana, South Carolina, and Virginia. It is here that the church can play a vital role and he suggests that:

1. The church can show the irrationality of racial prejudice,—that the idea of a "superior or inferior race of people is a myth."

2. The church can teach that the Negro does not want to dominate, but merely to live as an equal citizen with everyone else.

3. The churches can translate the principle of brotherhood into action.

4. The church can teach that man must devote his life to following God, not the prejudices of men.

5. The church must remove segregation from its own institution. Dean Liston Pope of Yale Divinity School has said: "The church is the most segregated major institution in American society. It has lagged behind the Supreme Court as the conscience of the nation on questions of race, and it has fallen far behind trade unions, factories, schools, department stores . . . and most other major areas of human association as far as the achievement of integration in its own life is concerned."

6. The church must take social action outside its own membership. It must strive for justice in housing, education, police protection, and in the city and state courts.

It is Martin Luther King's contention that the Negro, himself, must meet every act of barbarity by having one hundred more Negroes ready to present themselves as potential victims. He paraphrases the words of Gandhi: "We will match your capacity to inflict suffering with our capacity to endure suffering. We will meet your physical force with soul force. . . . Do to us what you will and we will still love you. . . . But we will wear you down by our capacity to suffer. And in winning our freedom we will so appeal to your heart and conscience that we will win you in the process."

Dr. King has been honored with sixty-five citations and awards for his work. As far back as 1957, he received the Social Justice Award of the Religion and Labor Foundation, and in 1961 at the Roosevelt Day Dinner, he received the Distinguished Award of Americans for Democratic Action. In a poll conducted by *Link Magazine*, he was ranked eleventh among world leaders who had contributed most to the advancement of freedom during 1959.

His life is like a beacon showing and inspiring us all to do more in our own occupations, in our communities, and in our religious affiliations.

XVI

YOUR LIFE IS YOUR MESSAGE

SCIENTIFIC ADVANCES HAVE made the world a very small sphere indeed. The entire globe can be circled in less than a day. We are now planning trips to the moon. Under these conditions it becomes more and more incredible that we do not have a world federal government. If this were achieved, it would mean that all nations and peoples would be brought into the organization, and elections would be based on population. Instead of this we are spending billions on weapons for mass murder and annihilation.

In many ways our ethical, moral and spiritual advances have not kept pace with our scientific achievements.

Lewis Mumford, the world-renowned writer, says: "Within a bare decade the United States has built up a huge vested interest in mass extermination. . . . There are tens of thousands of individual scientists and technicians engaged in nuclear, bacteriological, and chemical research to increase the range and effectiveness of these lethal agents, though we boast we already have a stockpile of nuclear weapons capable of wiping out the entire planet."

Science Service reported in 1962 that 800,000 children and adults are accidentally poisoned each year in the United States. Aspirin, alcohol, and barbiturates cause many poisonings, some of these not accidental. This indicates that we are doing very little to prevent these tragedies.

Charles A. Wells, the religious leader, stated in *Between the Lines* of February 15, 1962, that the United States Marines helped to set up "the brutal, benighted Somoza family dictatorship in Nicaragua." He went on to say, "Progress has been impaired and U.S. influence much damaged by the way we have favored the most despicable Latin American dictators. The U.S. military has followed the policy in these areas—as elsewhere—that, no matter how foul a tyrant may be, if he can be propped up on our side, we will arm him as part of our defense system. . . . The Pentagon has poured out weapons to such dictators as Batista in Cuba, Odria in Peru, Jiminez in Venezuela, Trujillo in the Dominican Republic, Somoza in Nicaragua, Stroessner in Paraguay, Peron in Argentina,—all names of ill repute. And a U.S. military mission (Marine Corps) is now retraining and rearming the forces of the dictator Duvalier in Haiti, of whom a leading expert on Latin America at Rutgers University, Robert J. Alexander, has written, 'He is the most tyrannical leader Haiti has had in this century . . . maintained by terrorist groups . . . who beat up, imprison, and kill the opponents of the regime.' "

John Gunther, writing in *Look* in 1962, pointed out that the United States unwisely supported "corrupt and reactionary governments in Turkey and South Korea." Because of our failures since the overthrow of the Tsar's regime, the communists have been expanding their world at the rate of fifty square miles an hour every day and night.

In many ways our society shows signs of moral arteriosclerosis. It has advanced scientifically over the years but stagnated morally. Christians know that Jesus taught us to "love our enemies," but in practice we violate our signed treaty obligations in trying to promote the overthrow of

Castro in Cuba, which turned out to be a disastrous fiasco, and we use every power at our command to prevent Red China from entering the United Nations. As Dr. Erich Fromm says: "Why is America panicky? Because she has lost her spirituality."

General David M. Shoup, commandant of the Marine Corps, testifying before the U.S. Senate, warned against indoctrinating members of the Armed Forces with the "poison" of hatred. "Hate I consider is an internal sin. And hate is closely associated with fear. I think fear breeds defeatism, and that is a disease that we cannot afford in this country if we are going to maintain our position in the family of freedom-loving people. . . . Hatred resembles a rifle with a plugged barrel. The backfire is more dangerous than the shot." Yet we have built up hatred and fear of communists all over the United States.

I have always remembered the words of the great writer Leo Tolstoy: "Only those live who do good." But suppose we were to make a statistical analysis of the lives of the American people, determining what proportion of them are devoting all that they are and have to bettering our society and helping others? Jesus taught that the greatest sin consists in that which divides, in injustice and greed, and if a single member of the human family is in need, this should be our concern.

We are far down in the scale of character if we have false mental pictures of other people, of the "dangerous Reds", and of other races. President Eisenhower blasted our society when he said: "Every gun that is made, every warship launched, every rocket fired signifies, in the final sense, a theft from those who hunger and are not fed, those who are cold and are not clothed."

Albert Einstein summed up the challenge which we face

in our time by saying: "Try not to become a man of success, but rather try to become a man of value. He is considered successful in our day who gets more out of life than he puts in. But a man of value will give more than he receives."

Our society is a constant challenge to us to reform and change it. As Roger Babson says: "When America's keenest minds are using newspapers, magazines, movies, and radios to entice youths to drink whiskey, smoke more cigarettes, and make heroes of criminals, these youths should be given the other side of the argument from someone."

If we study our society as it really is, we would do well to ponder the statement of President John F. Kennedy: "The question for our time is not whether all men are brothers . . . [but] whether we have the strength and the will to make the brotherhood of man the guiding principle of our lives."

In the chapters in this book, we have seen what some of the outstanding leaders of our generation have done. Do we realize that their lives are a flaming challenge to us? Are we willing to face this in our lives? Are we conscious of the fact that we will pass through this world but once, and that if we are ever going to begin to do good, instead of selfishly following the road to material success, *we must do it now?*

Can we not take the aspirations, the achievements of these men as a yardstick to measure our own lives? Each one of us has different abilities, different backgrounds, but the fundamental question is whether we are doing all we can with the capabilities we have.

Make a chart of the way you spend your time twenty-four hours a day and seven days a week. How much time is spent unselfishly for others? How much time is spent help-

ing the underprivileged, the needy, and the exploited? What happens to our money in the course of a year? What percentage is spent for charity and religious work? Do we plan to dedicate all our money to worthwhile causes when we die?

In colleges, the authorities sometimes use an "intelligence" test which determines your intelligence quotient or I.Q. Now, suppose we weigh our own lives in the light of the adventures of the men recorded in this book.

Suppose we had been born on a farm in Russia during the tyrannical regime of the Tsar, as Khrushchev was, what would we have accomplished in our lives?

Suppose we had grown up as a boy in Florida, as Raymond Robins did? Would we have been willing to go into the mines and champion justice for the miners with a consequent loss of job? If we had later come into possession of a third of a million dollars, would we have used it as well as he did?

Sir Wilfred Grenfell, when he graduated from medical school, asked to be sent where there were no doctors and where he could give his life for others. Are we willing to "go and do likewise?"

Harry Emerson Fosdick and Rabbi Stephen S. Wise spent all their lives leading others forward on the road to serving society and human brotherhood. John R. Mott devoted his entire career to serving the cause of Christ around the world. Mahatma Gandhi gave up all his property and lived in poverty that he might win freedom for the Indian people.

We are living in the most dangerous period in all human history. One third of the people of the world are living on less than one dollar per week. In facing up to the crucial problems of our time, it is imperative that we discard our

own little plans and narrow ideas and confront the actualities of the world scene. The struggle today is that of winning the minds and hearts of men on the intellectual, moral, spiritual and ideological planes. It is a battle for the minds and hearts of men.

We cannot win this contest by guns, planes, and nuclear weapons. We need to see that the two-fifths of mankind that are ignorant, diseased, and hungry are helped with schools, hospitals, and good food. We need to win both freedom and justice for all peoples. Another world war, if it comes, will mean the end of civilization as we know it. We should do more to implement that humanitarian ideal, *let us do everything for others, rather than for ourselves.*

What will you do to build international good will and friendship in every country around the world? Stop, look, listen, for the hour is late! Won't you start now to give everything you have to the cause of justice, liberty, and peace?